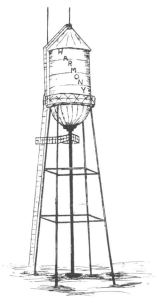

The Amish
of Harmony

D0006557

Collected and written
by Drucilla Milne
Harmony, Minnesota

Artist

Emeline Dahl, age 85, lives on a farm north of Harmony. She is known as an artist whose talents range from portraits to landscapes and still life. For many years she has lived near her Amish neighbors. Her son farms the land she still lives on.

Copyright 1993   Printed by Davies Printing Co., Rochester, MN   1993
6th Printing

ISBN: 0-9638637-0-3

Preface

Rumor has it that, when the Amish voiced an interest in this area, they were told by the first real estate agent they dealt with, "Those Norwegians will never accept you." I would venture to say that most of the residents of the Harmony area are not Norwegians, but just folks who want to live "in Harmony" with their English (as the Amish call anyone outside their community) and Amish neighbors. No matter what our ethnic background, as a whole we are people who have a love for Harmony. This story has been told many times and is the basis of the community's name, "Harmony":

In the southeastern corner of Minnesota, just north of the border with Iowa in Fillmore County, sits a small rural town which, in its early years from the 1860s, was called Greenfield Prairie. The stagecoach was the mode of travel in those early days. A few years later, when the train moved into the north end of Greenfield Prairie, the town began to grow north toward the railroad. The residents of this new community felt a desire to rename it. A meeting was called during which there was a great deal of discussion and discord as to what the new community should be called. One observer, tiring of the bickering, stood up and said, "Let us have harmony here!"[1] I chose to name my book "The Amish of Harmony" because harmony is what I feel for the town and the people.

---

[1] *Memories of Early Years of Harmony* by Anna Aaberg Jacobson, 1956.

Acknowledgements

I could never have put this material together without the information I gathered from a number of people from both Amish and English lifestyles.

My first thanks goes to my family for their encouragement and patience, and also to friends who encouraged me and did all the right things to keep me going.

Thank you to Martha King, an editor at Honeywell Inc., who helped me with the preliminary steps required for the writing process and for doing the first editing.

A special thank you to a friend and community librarian, Paula Michel, for giving unselfishly of her free time in doing the final editing. Her assistance in searching and finding resource material was very helpful.

Kristi Shuck is a student at Harmony High School and the daughter of Dr. Gerald and Shirley Shuck. She began to transcribe the material onto computer disks for me two years ago as a high school freshman. The fortitude, unselfish devotion, and care she gave to my project was much appreciated.

The Fillmore County Journal has worked closely with me in a friendly and professional manner transferring Kristi's disks into book form and doing picture layouts. Their employees, expecially Gretchen Bollweg, gave of their talents and time as freely as business would allow.

I am indebted to Mavis Johnson who read the manuscript on short notice and offered comments from a reader's point of view.

Sincere thanks to Joan Michel, Nancy Overby, Lynda Koliha, and Sherry Hines, who did small favors which were enormously helpful.

I cannot forget my Amish friends who by lending an ear to the written material, gave this book its authenticity. It has been my pleasure to work with such caring people.

I wish also to extend thanks to:
  Millicent Johnson (collector of Harmony's history);
  Members of the Harmony Area Cancer Support Group;
  George Milne (retired Clerk of Court, Fillmore County);
  Toni Scott (student at the University of Wisconsin-Stout, Menomonie, Wisconsin) for children's mouse, baby in cradle, and twins in a cradle illustrations;
  Sharen Storhoff, for photos of Old Barn Resort;
  Lonnie Yoder and the Historical Society of the Mennonite Church of Kalona, Iowa, and its president, Lester Miller, for the *Mennonite Church History Chart*.

Table of Contents

The Amish of Harmony

Part I

Getting to Know the Amish of Harmony

Introduction

This book is about one particular community, not a general description of the Amish people. Because the Old Order Amish live in a close community, there is limited opportunity for Englishers to know or understand them and their culture. This book introduces readers to the Amish as people, in hopes of dispelling some common myths and misconceptions about them, and serves as a bridge between the Amish and English.

I have tried to write this book in a way which will not hurt, offend or cause embarrassment. The Amish do not like to be singled out in stories or be quoted. I have used court records and newspapers as a source of information plus personal knowledge and experience. I am not infallible. It is like an Amish quilt; you'll usually find an error. It can then be said that it is put there to remind us of the fallibility of man.

I have shared my writings with the Amish. Having put it together as accurately as I can, I then went to them and read what I'd written. One Amish person, feeling that I had been too explicit, told me very simply, "Shorten it up."

Drucilla Milne

My New Neighbors

My first reaction to my new Amish neighbors was to observe. They were as strange to me as I thought I was to them. Maybe more so for me because they had had English (as they call all outsiders) neighbors before. I had never had Amish neighbors and therefore didn't know what to expect. I soon found them to be friendly and easy to get along with. Their ways were different than ours and I accepted that. I can best illustrate this with a story: I'd stopped in to one of my Amish friend's homes, as I often did, to visit and to pick up eggs. I happened to arrive right at mealtime. The family of five were seated on wooden benches (without backs) around the long harvest table enjoying their meal. I apologized. "I'm always forgetting your time is different from ours!" (They stay on standard time when we go on daylight savings time.) My friend laughed, "You probably think we're funny." I laughed too and replied, "No funnier than you must think we are."

A new Amish homestead.

One of my family's earliest experiences with how helpful our Amish neighbors could be came in the spring of 1977. We had heard that they would tear down old barns and reuse the lumber that is salvageable. Our old barn had been built in 1926 and from all appearances looked pretty good from the outside; it still held a good coat of paint but was in poor repair. My husband wanted it torn down. He approached our Amish neighbors and asked if they'd tear it down, the agreement being that we would share the lumber. They also got the hayfork, pulleys, and track for a barn that was to be raised for a young couple just beginning to farm. Many Amish men and boys came to help and our barn went down quickly. We thought it was great. Not knowing at that time that the Amish believe in no graven images (Deuteronomy 5:8 and the second commandment), I went out with a camera and took a picture to record how our barn came down. One young boy backed away into the barn door and I heard him make a comment about my taking a picture. It was only later that I became more familiar with their beliefs on this subject, which I discuss in more detail in the chapter entitled "Graven Images."

Throughout our area can be seen barns of new lumber as well as old weathered lumber. On one of their farms, the Amish disassembled an old barn and rebuilt it, using both the lumber that was salvageable from the old barn and some new lumber, on the existing foundation. While we recycle plastic, glass, and newsprint, the Amish recycle barns and other buildings. An Amish barn is easily identified because it is not painted in the same year it is built. Painting is held off to let any green barn boards weather.

New Beginnings

In Wayne County, Ohio, in the early 1970s the Amish were being crowded out commercially as well as by over-population. It was time to begin looking for new land, to begin a new community of Amish. Three trips were made into areas of Wisconsin and/or Minnesota. The name of the real estate agent was found in an ad in *The Budget*. (This is the weekly paper serving the Amish-Mennonite communities through the Americas. It is published in Sugarcreek, Ohio.) In August of 1973, four men traveled by bus to Austin, Minnesota. They were met at the hotel by the real estate agent. The first land they were shown was in the northern part of Fillmore County. On one trip they traveled from La Crosse, Wisconsin, through Canton and Harmony townships. They were impressed by what they saw: wooded timber areas for building and for fuel, springs (a water source) for animals and cooling milk, small acreage farms, good soil with good drainage. Land prices were reasonable (approximately $300 to $700/acre). The Amish men asked to be put into contact with a real estate agent from this area.

Those who first purchased land had farms for sale in Ohio and/or had cash down payments. A very few had mineral rights to natural gas or coal. Most farms purchased were 80 to 160 acres. On plat maps the ideal one-family farm appears to be 80 acres. Larger farms are eventually split and made into two and three-

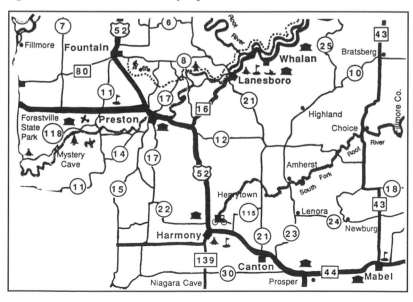

family farms. The Ohio Amish began moving into areas of Canton and Harmony townships in February or March of 1974. Their farm machinery and horses were shipped by freight train. While visiting throughout this Old Order community, I have observed and have discovered some interesting differences from our modern way of life. I can only attempt to describe these and cannot say this is true of all Amish. When a new community begins, there are Amish who come in from other states. This order of Amish near Harmony were of the least progressive or oldest order. Some Amish moving into this new community may have been a little more progressive in their ways but had to adhere to changes. Changes could be seen, heard, and felt.

One day I drove into the yard of a newly purchased farm. I could see a T.V. antenna leaning against the house. (They have no electricity and disconnect current.) The outline of shutters which had been removed from the windows because they are considered decorative and of "our world" could still be seen. The creek that ran near the house and through the pasture was running well, as we'd had several nice rains. (The creek is used for refrigeration, cooling products). The carriage horses were grazing in the pasture and a black horsedrawn carriage could be seen in the yard. As I approached the house I could hear singing. It was the clear voice of a young girl singing the lyrics in German. (They speak German in the homes). She'd gone to the creek to get a covered metal container, where it had been cooling. As she approached the house she stilled her singing.

Outside the home, in the yard, sat a Maytag gasoline-operated washing machine. A few feet away was a large cast iron cauldron about three feet in diameter and twenty-two inches deep.

It was set up on a stand so a wood fire could be built under it for heating water because the Amish have only cold running water in their homes. In the winter or when cold weather comes, washing machines are taken inside. The water for bathing and washing clothes will be heated inside in reservoirs on black woodburning stoves or in brick ovens built to support the large cast iron cauldron.

An outdoor toilet had been built near the home, as bathrooms and tubs are taken out. Many times an aluminum tub (much like those seen in Western movies), can be seen hanging in summer kitchens. (This small building is used to keep the heat out of the main house.)

As I approached the big porch running across the width of the house, I greeted my Amish friends. The screened windows were open and they were busy making reed baskets of all shapes, sizes, and colors. On a long table lay reed snowflakes, and hearts. The mother and daughter were working the long water-soaked lengths of colored reed. The father was finishing a basket handle and frame onto which the reed is woven. It would soon be meal-time, so my visit was short. We shared some humor and conversation and I felt I had entered another time zone. I enjoy their culture and the families I've come to know.

The families that first year of 1974 were few. Only a handful of children were of school age. They were taught in a small room off the sitting room of one of these family homes. A one-room school was provided later as more families eventually moved in. They do not attend our public schools. By 1993 there were 6 one-room schools (there had been 7 schools but one closed) in this community of 90 families, with an average of 5 to 6 children per family.

The Amish, of course, had a long history before ever arriving in Harmony. They endured many moves and many hardships since their beginnings in Europe. Much has been written on the historical beginnings of this Christian group and can be found in more detail in those sources.[2] Briefly, the Amish group was originally part of the Mennonites, a group which broke away from a radical group of Anabaptists (believing in adult baptism) during the Protestant Reformation in 1525 in Zurich, Switzerland. The founder of the Mennonites was named Menno Simons, a Catholic priest from Holland. The Amish are sometimes called Amish-Mennonite because they were originally part of the Mennonites but broke way during the reformation in 1693. Their founder, Jacob Amman, was a Swiss Mennonite bishop. These groups were severely persecuted for their beliefs, and in the 18th century to escape this persecution the Amish began immigrating to America. The Mennonites had begun to immigrate in the 17th

---

[2] Hostetler, John A. *Amish Society.* Baltimore, MD, Johns Hopkins University Press 1980, Chapter 2, pages 25-49.

century. A diagram of the history of these groups is found on the following fold out page.[3]

Mennonite Church History Chart

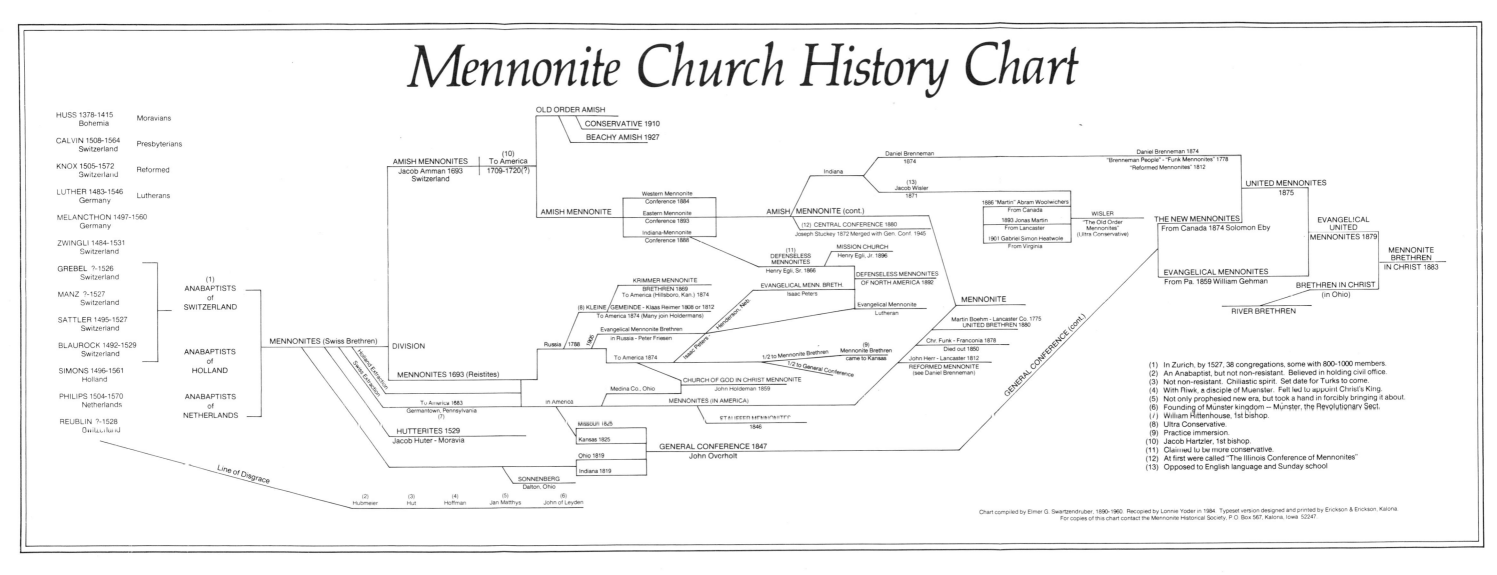

HUSS 1378-1415
Bohemia — Moravians

CALVIN 1508-1564
Switzerland — Presbyterians

KNOX 1505-1572
Switzerland — Reformed

LUTHER 1483-1546
Germany — Lutherans

MELANCTHON 1497-1560
Germany

ZWINGLI 1484-1531
Switzerland

GREBEL ?-1526
Switzerland

MANZ ?-1527
Switzerland

SATTLER 1495-1527
Switzerland

BLAUROCK 1492-1529
Switzerland

SIMONS 1496-1561
Holland

PHILIPS 1504-1570
Netherlands

REUBLIN ?-1528
Switzerland

(1) ANABAPTISTS of SWITZERLAND

ANABAPTISTS of HOLLAND

ANABAPTISTS of NETHERLANDS

MENNONITES (Swiss Brethren)

DIVISION

MENNONITES 1693 (Reistites)

Holland Extinction
Swiss Extinction

To America 1683
Germantown, Pennsylvania
(7)

HUTTERITES 1529
Jacob Huter - Moravia

Line of Disgrace

OLD ORDER AMISH

CONSERVATIVE 1910

BEACHY AMISH 1927

AMISH MENNONITES
Jacob Amman 1693
Switzerland

(10) To America
1709-1720(?)

AMISH MENNONITE

Western Mennonite
Conference 1884

Eastern Mennonite
Conference 1893

Indiana-Mennonite
Conference 1888

KRIMMER MENNONITE
BRETHREN 1869
To America (Hillsboro, Kan.) 1874

(8) KLEINE GEMEINDE - Klaas Reimer 1808 or 1812
To America 1874 (Many join Holdermans)

Evangelical Mennonite Brethren
in Russia - Peter Friesen

Russia 1788   1905

To America 1874

Medina Co., Ohio

In America

Missouri 1825

Kansas 1825

Ohio 1819

Indiana 1819

SONNENBERG
Dalton, Ohio

Daniel Brenneman
1874

Indiana

AMISH / MENNONITE (cont.)

(12) CENTRAL CONFERENCE 1880
Joseph Stuckey 1872 Merged with Gen. Conf. 1945

(11)
DEFENSELESS
MENNONITES
Henry Egli, Sr. 1866

MISSION CHURCH
Henry Egli, Jr. 1896

EVANGELICAL MENN. BRETH.
Isaac Peters

Isaac Peters, Henderson, Neb.

CHURCH OF GOD IN CHRIST MENNONITE
John Holdeman 1859

MENNONITES (IN AMERICA)

STAUFFER MENNONITES
1846

GENERAL CONFERENCE 1847
John Overholt

(13)
Jacob Wisler
1871

1886 "Martin" Abram Woolwichers
From Canada

1893 Jonas Martin
From Lancaster

1901 Gabriel Simon Heatwole
From Virginia

DEFENSELESS MENNONITES
OF NORTH AMERICA 1892

Evangelical Mennonite
Lutheran

MENNONITE

Martin Boehm - Lancaster Co. 1775
UNITED BRETHREN 1880

1/2 to Mennonite Brethren

1/2 to General Conference

(9)
Mennonite Brethren
came to Kansas

Chr. Funk - Franconia 1878
Died out 1850

John Herr - Lancaster 1812
REFORMED MENNONITE
(see Daniel Brenneman)

GENERAL CONFERENCE (cont.)

WISLER
"The Old Order
Mennonites"
(Ultra Conservative)

Daniel Brenneman 1874
"Brenneman People" - "Funk Mennonites" 1778
"Reformed Mennonites" 1812

UNITED MENNONITES
1875

THE NEW MENNONITES
From Canada 1874 Solomon Eby

EVANGELICAL MENNONITES
From Pa. 1859 William Gehman

RIVER BRETHREN

EVANGELICAL
UNITED
MENNONITES 1879

BRETHREN IN CHRIST
(in Ohio)

MENNONITE
BRETHREN
IN CHRIST 1883

(1) In Zurich, by 1527, 38 congregations, some with 800-1000 members.
(2) An Anabaptist, but not non-resistant. Believed in holding civil office.
(3) Not non-resistant. Chiliastic spirit. Set date for Turks to come.
(4) With Riwk, a disciple of Muenster. Felt led to appoint Christ's King.
(5) Not only prophesied new era, but took a hand in forcibly bringing it about.
(6) Founding of Münster kingdom — Münster, the Revolutionary Sect.
(7) William Rittenhouse, 1st bishop.
(8) Ultra Conservative.
(9) Practice immersion.
(10) Jacob Hartzler, 1st bishop.
(11) Claimed to be more conservative.
(12) At first were called "The Illinois Conference of Mennonites"
(13) Opposed to English language and Sunday school

(2) Hubmeier   (3) Hut   (4) Hoffman   (5) Jan Matthys   (6) John of Leyden

Chart compiled by Elmer G. Swartzendruber, 1890-1960. Recopied by Lonnie Yoder in 1984. Typeset version designed and printed by Erickson & Erickson, Kalona.
For copies of this chart contact the Mennonite Historical Society, P.O. Box 567, Kalona, Iowa 52247.

[3] *Mennonite Church History Chart*, 1890-1960, compiled by Elmer G. Swartzendruber. Recopied by Lonnie Yoder in 1984. Type set version designed and printed by Erickson and Erickson, Kalona, Iowa. The primary source for the Anabaptist-Mennonite portion of this chart is a chart in *An Introduction to Mennonite History* by Cornelius J. Duck (editor) and published by Herald Press (the publishing house of the Mennonite Church), 1967 edition.

Living in the World but not Being of the World

I have had difficulty in trying to explain the concept of the Amish belief of "living in the world but not being of the world." I believe many Englishers have problems understanding this and so I will try to explain how the Amish perceive this way of life and how they live it. The concept is based on the Bible and can be found in verses such as I John 2:15-18, Rom 12:2, Rom 13-18, Mt 6:24, James 4:6, Prov 22:20, I Cor 7:31.

In I John 2:15-17, it says "Do not love the world or the things in the world. If anyone loves the world, love for the Father is not in him." "For all that is in the world, the lust of the flesh and the lust of the eyes and the pride of life, is not of the Father but is of the world." "And the world passes away, and the lust of it; but he who does the will of God abides forever."

The Amish believe that these Bible passages and others call them to a life of separation and self-denial. For example Rom 12:1-2 says to present our bodies as a living sacrifice, holy and acceptable to God, what is good and acceptable and perfect. These bible verses are paraphrased in The One Bible Commentary, (Edited by J.R. Dummelow) as such: Rom 12:1-2, vs 1— "God's redeeming love should be answered by the true and spiritual ritual service of a life of purity and self-denial and work for God." Vs 2—"Do not follow the fashions and customs of the worldly society around you, but let your ways of thinking be so

Living in the world.

changed by the Holy Spirit that you look for and recognize God's will and love to do it."

This, for example, is why sameness in dress, home furnishings and livelihood are required, taking away the lures of worldly ways concerning fashion, material goals, and those status symbols of wealth and prominence. They are continually working towards the good of the Amish community by setting guidelines to ward off the ways of the world. Therefore, a life of separateness is stressed. They see living in a modern world as a continually ongoing battle.

In order for them to remain as the least progressive, Old Order Amish, they must have guidelines. Their ordnung is the result of these guidelines. *Ordnung* means unwritten rules and regulations; many times it is not written down in a book of law but known throughout the community. Guidelines are discussed by church elders, bishops, deacons, and ministers. They help to regulate church members' conduct in confronting a modern world. This ordnung varies from region to region, state to state, and group to group.

Something as simple to Englishers as a ride in a car becomes an issue to be weighed with great concern or gravity. It can become a threat to their way of life. Let me explain. To accept a ride that is offered as a pleasure can be too convenient or frivolous and therefore unnecessary. This is discouraged. Yet if a ride is needed for a doctor's appointment to a far city or town, the Amish will hire a car or van or will use our bus or train systems. This is considered a temporary necessity. It isn't feasible to travel by horse and buggy to far places. Work, health, funerals, weddings and such are considered in this same category.

Many elders feel travel for vacations to see God's country and natural sights is too frivolous. Others feel that as long as God created these natural sights it is okay. However they never approve of commercial entertainment such as Disneyland or Disneyworld, because these are too worldly. Zoos are acceptable but not amusement parks.

I can best illustrate this in the following way: Imagine there is a line drawn in the dirt representing the Amish way. On either side of this line, imagine a modern world. To take one step off this line to the left or right is okay—but not ten steps—and they must always remember to come back to that straight line of self denial.

An example of limiting progress is seen in their woodworking shops, many times located on 1- 2- and 3-family farms. The very modern machinery is driven by a diesel engine which propels a drive shaft that runs along the floor near all their equipment. A belt is attached to the drive shaft and to the machine being used—so

Belt driven modern machinery in a furniture craft shop.

A furniture craft shop.

they need no electricity! Electricity would bring too many lures of a modern world.* Woodworking shops have been allowed only because of lack of farm land.

Woodburning stoves are used for heating and cooking. There are no central heating systems. There is only cold running water in the homes but it is run directly into the house with a gasoline engine attached to a windmill pump jack. When there is no wind it can still pump water into the homes. Some Amish run water into their homes by using gravity. A tank is placed high in an insulated building and pumped full of water with the aid of a gasoline or diesel engine, rather than with a pressure pump run by electricity as Englishers do.

Water is pumped in to the house by a windmill. It is wind generated, or a gas engine attached to a pumpjack generates running water.

---

*For the same reason, they do not use modern farm machinery but stay with the traditional horse farming method.

The Amish do not conduct business on Sundays or religious holidays. These are the Lord's Days and are honored as such. I have known people who came great distances for a tour or to pick up furniture on a Sunday or holiday, only to be disappointed because they had not written ahead to make arrangements.

Their weekly paper, *The Budget*, carries only Amish-and Mennonite-related news. It contains no national news. This is again considered too worldly.

Low German or "Pennsylvania Dutch" is spoken in Amish homes as another form of remaining separate. Yet the English language is taught in Amish schools, because they do live in an English-speaking country.

One day while visiting at the first Amish home allowing tourists to stop I observed this: As we women were visiting in English, the Amish husband approached and spoke to his wife. They spoke in German to each other but, when addressing me, spoke English. It seemed a very natural thing to do. Also usage of "your way, our way, your people, our people" is very common; it calls attention to the separateness of the two cultures.

One bishop gave me this example of progressiveness: It's like falling off a roof; you can't stop the fall. (Just as a fall cannot be stopped, neither can progress.) So they do pick and choose with caution and leadership. Choosing can lead to gradual change or snowball into many changes.

Small items for sale in furniture craft shop.

23

The Amish are not backwards or ignorant. They appear backwards in our eyes but this is their choice of lifestyle. They only take from "our world" what is not threatening to "their way" of life. Therefore they will use our telephones, modes of travel, hospitals, clinics, doctors, and medical knowledge for health. These choices take them temporarily into "our world."

Amish do not believe in purchasing health, fire, wind, or life insurances. Families give their hands in service, bringing in food, and/or giving both monetary and emotional support in all times of crisis. They sustain each other as a community of God.

Ways of Separating
(from the world at large)

1. The Amish speak German in their homes and learn English only after they begin to attend school.

2. They have one room schoolhouses, and they attend through eighth grade only.

3. Dress styles and home furnishings are identical within the group, promoting sameness and eliminating the symbols of fashion and material wealth.

4. Woodburning stoves are used for cooking and heating. Amish homes have no central heating systems.

5. Electricity is not used.

6. They use horses to farm and for local travel.

7. *The Budget* is a weekly paper that publishes Amish-Mennonite news to communities across North America. The Amish take no other national news papers.

8. Church is held in their homes.

9. Amish have their own cemeteries.

10. There are no nursing homes. Care for aged relatives is within the family or they have a home on the same farm site as their children.

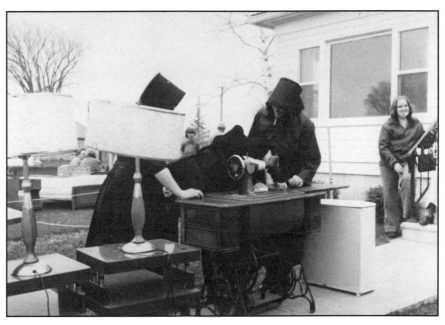

This photo was taken at an auction sale in the spring of 1978. The person who took this picture was unaware of the Amish belief, "You shall have no graven images." (Deut 5:8)

Graven Images

The Ten Commandments provide a guideline to leading a Christian life. The second commandment, Deut 5:8 reads: "You shall not make for yourself a graven image, or any likeness of anything that is in heaven above, or that is on the earth beneath, or that is in the water under the earth." This is the basis for the Amish not wanting pictures taken. It is also the reason the Amish have no faces on dolls, no mirrors in homes, (only a small mirror for shaving) and do not own or use cameras or any of our mechanisms for capturing images. This is one of the reasons I give a controlled tour. They (and we) would prefer that no pictures of any kind be taken since the camera itself is offensive. We encourage people to respect their culture and beliefs.

The following stories relate to the belief in no graven images:

Cultivating Corn

I witnessed an Amish man who was cultivating his corn with a three-hitch horse-drawn cultivator actually getting down off the cultivator and lying flat in the row of corn beside the cultivator. Why? Because a van was driving slowly by and he assumed pictures were being taken. They were not! However tourists are often under the assumption that, as long as a distance is kept or no faces are shown, taking pictures is okay. But the camera alone is offensive.

Children's Hands

One mother wrote back to Harmony after the family had moved to Michigan. She wanted us to see how the children had grown so she had traced each child's hand on paper and mailed it to us.

Little Reuben (5 years old) drew a friendly smiling face and printed his name on his hand.

27

Calendar

In one home, I observed a calendar picture covered with construction paper. It had a "graven image," but the numbers and spaces on the calendar were large. Rather than discarding the whole calendar, they had covered the picture.

Black Sock Doll

I had a school bus of mixed races out on tour one day. The Amish children were as intrigued by these children as the English children were with the Amish. On my return trip to this same Amish household some days later, I noticed the small four-year-old Amish girl had a black sock doll with no face, dressed in Amish clothing. I asked where she got it. She replied, "I asked my grandma to make it for me." Later I found out the grandmother had put a white piece of cloth on the front of it. The little Amish girl removed it. She wanted a black-face doll.

Teddy Bear

Stuffed animals are not accepted by the Amish because of graven image. An English neighbor, knowing this, thought if she made a teddy bear without features it would be acceptable. She wanted to give the bear to an Amish child who had undergone much hospitalization. She thought a teddy bear's softness would give the child some comfort. When she presented the teddy bear to the child's parent, she was told it couldn't be accepted. She questioned this, "Why not?" She was told firmly, but as a friend, "Don't beg, it's graven image. Give it to one of your grandchildren." He didn't intend to give offense but was just stating a fact.

Sneaking a Close Up

On Highway 52, a lady had pulled over and stood behind her car, waiting for an approaching horse and buggy. She waited until the Amish buggy was almost to her before putting up her camera to snap a picture. Things began to happen in a series of events. First, the Amish lady in the buggy turned her head to the side, her wide brim black bonnet covering her face. Her husband pulled the reins sharply to the left, startling the horse and also turned his head and dipped his hat to the right trying to shield his face from the camera. He pulled around her car and proceeded on his way home. Luckily there was no on-coming traffic and this near-accident was avoided.

Part II

Life in an Amish Home

Homes and Home Furnishings

People and Clothing

Children

Old Order Amish Schools

Secrets (Courtship, Weddings, Birthing and Midwives)

Church in the Homes (Baptism, Communion, Funerals and Cemeteries)

Social Life (Barnraising and Quilting)

Homes and Home Furnishings

"No lines." I use this description for Amish homes, because when driving by you will see no electrical lines going to the house, unless it is rented or contracts of sale demand otherwise.

Young Amish men estimated the cost for what they had to buy for building a home at approximately $10,000 to $15,000. This includes windows, siding, shingles, roof and wall sheeting, sheet rock, hardware, insulation, cement foundation, and oak inlaid floors.

The house would consist of five bedrooms with closets, a large main room (or family room), a large kitchen (no built-in cupboards), a pantry and back entry, and an open porch extending across the front of the house. Windows are Amish-made and lumber is home-sawed pine or purchased pine. Sometimes a frolic is arranged to help with building. These gatherings are called a shed frolic, house frolic, or barn frolic. Why? Because they are considered social events as well as work-related.

A new Amish homestead. This large house was moved in by housemovers. A well was drilled and a barnraising organized. The barn was built using recycled lumber from our barn.

One family built an addition onto their home using material they'd obtained from an old house in a town nearby. A large kitchen, an entry and a basement to be used as a summer kitchen, a laundry room and root cellar were added. A large open porch was added to one end of the house. They also shingled the entire roof. The siding would be added, but it would have to wait until they could afford it. Vinyl siding is used and they would side only one side at a time as earnings permit. Tourists often ask, "Isn't vinyl siding too modern for their life style?" Amish say it's the practical way to go and saves painting costs. Whereas electricity is too threatening to their lifestyle because it causes change, adding siding doesn't cause any subsequent changes.

A"Recycled" Amish home. A house was torn down and the material was used to add on to this house.

Home Furnishings

Main room or family room

The curtains throughout the home are dark blue and are gathered onto a string or hang straight using a loop at each corner attached to a nail or hook.

There are no pictures or wall decorations. A shelf may hold a clock or colored glass, a cup rack with pegs displaying utensils or cups, and a calendar may be seen.

The wood box (oak or painted) is used for sitting as well as wood storage.

There are two hickory rocking chairs, padded with homemade cushions pieced in dark colors.

Usually there is a serviceable table with two straight-back chairs, a secretary and desk chair with casters. There may also be one or two Singer sewing machines used for needle crafts, clothing and mending. There is a daybed in the main room with a pieced and quilted covering, also in dark colors. Most of the furniture is oak and is Amish-made. Kerosene lamps with reflectors can be seen attached to the walls.

A large black woodburning stove is located near one wall at the center of this room.

33

Kitchen

Kitchens are large, containing a long harvest table with two benches, a dry sink (used as a work bench), a hand pump and sink or a cold water faucet and sink (no hot water faucets). Water is brought into the house from the windmill with a pump run by a gas engine. A hutch holds dishes.

A black woodburning range is used to heat and cook for the family.

Bedrooms

Bedrooms are furnished very simply with a bed and bureau or chest of drawers and sometimes a nightstand or table. On the beds are pieced quilts in dark colors, sometimes with a white, blue, black or dark green pleated skirt under the quilt. Some Amish make homemade feather pillows; however beds and mattresses are sometimes obtained at auctions.

Clotheslines are often seen on pulleys coming from windmills or high on buildings, enabling the Amish women to stand on the open porch and hang up clothes or take them down. Clothes racks are used indoors.

Household Remedies

Plugged Drain: Bleach will open it. Let set a few hours and then rinse with hot water.

Warmer Floor Temperature: Lay styrofoam down before pouring cement floor.

Scorched Prayer Kapp or Apron: Dampen a white handkerchief with hydrogen peroxide, place over scorch and iron. Works on whites.

Garden Remedies

On a hot, dry summer day in 1988, I drove into the Amish yard and noticed in the garden large three-pound coffee cans buried near the tomato plants. I was told that holes were poked in the bottom of these cans so they could be filled with water, watering closer to the roots. Coffee cans are used early in the spring as protection from the frost, covering the small plants and using the plastic lid. Later the lid is removed and the can supports the plant stem as it grows. Also, a rag can be wrapped at the base of vine plants with the loose end submerged in a pan of water, siphoning moisture to them. To prevent weeds in asparagus, the plant can be sprinkled with salt. Asparagus is a type of sea weed. Putting one package of yeast in one quart of warm water is very helpful in growing healthier tomatoes.

People and Clothing

Colors

Colors themselves are not offensive to the Amish. For example, they use the color red to paint their barns, and orange vests and an orange cloth tied around a black felt hat are often used during the hunting season. I've seen this on young men tearing down a dirt road in pursuit of a deer. I have also seen colorful towels, blankets, and other linens purchased by Amish women at second-hand outlet stores or at auctions. Blankets and linens are not worn but put to a practical use.

One Amish woman bought a pink electric blanket, and then clipped the corners and pulled out the wiring. I have even known of sleeping bags being unzipped and used as insulated blankets. But bright colors are never used in clothing.

The quilts of bright colors, pieced in many patterns, are made for the English. Amish quilts are made of the same colors used in their clothing.

While giving tours I have heard people refer to the Amish clothing as costumes. (Webster's Dictionary defines costume: "dress peculiar.") Peculiar to whom? These clothing patterns have been handed down from generation to generation. Sameness and simplicity are a way of life.

I have found these people of the Amish faith to be very tolerant. My good intentions have sometimes been my downfall. For example: After trying to remember the names of seven children in one family, I said in exasperation, "If they didn't all dress alike it would be easier to remember the names," to which the young mother replied, "Just because we dress alike doesn't mean we look alike! Look at the faces."

Women's and Girls' Clothing

I Peter 3:3-4: "Let not yours be the outward adorning with braided hair, decoration of gold, and wearing of robes, but let it be the hidden person of the heart with the imperishable jewel of a gentle and quiet spirit, which in God's sight is very precious." These verses describe the basis for the Amish choice of clothing.

Colors for clothing consist of the dark shades: blue, black, brown, dark green, teal blue, burgundy, or gray. Colors and dress length can vary among different orders of Amish. There may also be a slight difference in prayer "kapps." There are no buttons on

37

girls' or women's clothing; rather, they will use hook and eye closures, straight pins and safety pins. Little girls have buttons down the backs of their dresses for practical reasons and these buttons are not decorative.

Girls and women wear capes and clothing with no collars or lapels. Both men's and women's shoes are black. Many men, women, and children go barefoot as soon as weather permits. No jewelry is worn for ornamentation.

Boys' and Men's Clothing

Men's and boys' clothing have no lapels or collars. Coats, jackets, and shirts have a narrow standing collar with hooks and eyes. Undergarments and trousers (called "broadfall trousers") have button closures. On clotheslines, waistlines look large because pockets hang straight out at the waist. Pockets fold in and then button to a bib. Suspenders are of leather or cloth with two buttons at the back and front.

Little boys who are under school age wear a dress until they are toilet trained. Then they begin to wear trousers.

Pants and jackets are denim. Blue shirts or dark shirts are for daily wear. Black pants, vests or jackets and white collarless shirts with two buttons at the neck are worn on Church Sundays.

Women's and Girls' Headcoverings

I Corinthians 11:5: "But any women who prays or prophesies with her head unveiled dishonors her head — it is the same as if her head were shaven." (This Bible verse explains why Amish women wear a prayer kapp.) Women and girls wear prayer kapps of white and sometimes black. Mothers and older girls generally wear white prayer kapps. Small girls and young girls wear dark kapps. Why? Probably because they don't show the soil and because they don't have to be pleated. White prayer kapps are heavily starched and pinched into tiny pleats that are ironed in with a heavy cast iron which is heated on a woodburning stove and then clipped to a handle. A black pleated prayer Kapp is worn on Church Sundays by young unmarried girls.

Large wide-brimmed black bonnets which tie under the chin and extend over the face and cover the neck, are worn by all women when away from home, traveling, or working in the sun.

I Corinthians 11:15-16 says, "But if any women has long hair, is it her pride? For her hair is given to her for a covering." (Amish women have long hair and are not to cut it. However it may break off from much pinning and the weight of the hair.) Older girls and women roll their hair and use hair pins to hold it in place. Young girls braid their hair and very small girls with fine hair have it braided into many braids using string to give each braid consistency and firmness. At one home I visited, a ten year old girl's prayer kapp was above her ears. Her hair was very long and thick. I patted the top of her head and it felt as soft as a pillow. Her mother said she needed to make new prayer kapps to cover her ears.

On a Saturday before church Sunday, the young mother was busy washing her daughters' hair. The twelve year old girl's hair hung loose drying. It reached almost to the back of her knees. One tiny girl sat on the table; Mother had taken out the strings that had held her many braids and her short hair stuck out in all directions.

Later, as Mother was standing ironing, the two boys played on the floor opposite the kitchen with a farm set. The baby lay in the crib sleeping. Mother's hair was long and dark and tied in a wide blue yarn bow. She had washed the hair and it was drying loose. The yarn ribbon served to hold the hair from her face.

I also witnessed the Amish grandmother as she babysat, braiding the hair of her grandchild, a small girl of 1 1/2 or 2, into many braids tied with a string to hold the fine uneven lengths. The little girl was crying for all she was worth. Grandmother was firm but kind, and soon the job was done and a white prayer kapp put on.

Men's and Boys' Headcoverings

I Corinthians 11:4 says, "Any man who prays or prophesies with his head covered dishonors his head." This means they remove their head coverings for church.

Men and boys wear flat-top homemade straw hats in the summer. You will also see the male children with flat straw hats, worn out but still being worn. They cut the brim off and wear them as what I term "a kettle hat." In cooler weather a black felt hat is worn. Different orders of Amish have different sized brims and styles. In winter little boys wear a dark heavy headscarf over the ears and a black felt hat. Little baby boys wear black bonnets just as baby girls do, the difference being that baby girls have a white prayer kapp under it, while the boys wear just the bonnet.

Men's and Boys' Hair

I Corinthians 11:14 says, "Does not nature itself teach you that for a man to wear long hair is degrading to him?" Therefore Amish men keep the hair cut to just below the ears.

Beards

Men who are clean-shaven are not married. Those who have a trimmed beard covering only the jawline are baptized. A married man has a long flowing beard. The cheeks are clean-shaven and there is no moustache.

Children

On many Amish farms there is more than one home. There may be a son or daughter and his/her spouse and family, grandparents and sometimes great grandparents, aunts and uncles or great aunts and uncles, all living on the same farm but in separate homes. The children of all ages go in and out of these homes with the same ease as in the familiarity of their own home. I love to observe the children in this Amish community and their simpler life.

There are three homes on this farm. The railing and gate on the porch of one of those homes is not a decoration but a large playpen for smaller children.

I know one two-year-old who has three homes on the farm he is living on. He goes from grandma and grandpa's to aunt's to his own home and is welcomed in each. Each one gives loving attention as well as restrictions as to what he is allowed to do and have. The little ones go about in their dresses (both boys and girls wear dresses until they are toilet trained) in cloth diapers (no rubber pants) toddling hither and yon as mothers, aunts and grandparents (older brothers and sisters being in school) do their daily tasks. They may be washing clothes in the wash house, gardening, baking, canning, or sewing.

41

One day I went visiting to the home where a quilt was being made for a nephew of mine. The house had a wide-open porch with the garden and fruit trees just out front. A fence surrounded the yard with a gate at the front and one at the back. I went up onto the porch and knocked. I was greeted warmly and ushered into the large kitchen. At the dry sink stood a small girl with a dark prayer kapp on her head. She stood on a footstool washing dishes. Her two sisters, only a year or two older, were drying dishes and putting them away. It was a Saturday and Mother had done some baking just in case they should get company on Sunday (it was a visiting Sunday—church is every other Sunday). We went into the large parlor where I was shown some of the mother's projects and the pieces of the quilt and the progress she had already made. The baby sat on the bare wood floor where her small sister of 2 1/2 or 3 played with her. The child was hugging, playing with and nurturing the baby gently, which she had learned through observing.

The children's mother, as we sat visiting, had her small children standing quietly about her. As we visited her hands were busy entertaining the children in a quiet manner. She had a man's white handkerchief and was folding and pulling at it, first to shape a mouse, then a baby in a cradle, then twins in a cradle. Our conversation went on uninterrupted and the children were entertained and quietly satisfied.

Babies in a Cradle

1. Fold hankerchief in half at corners.

2. Roll corners #2 and #3 into each other until they meet in the middle.

3. While holding the rolled ends, pull the layers of 1a and 1b in opposite directions, split ting at the point until these are two babies in a cradle.

4. To make one baby in a cradle, roll the two rolls up to the top and then repeat step #3.

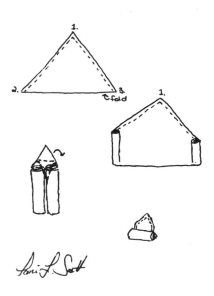

Mouse

1. Fold hankerchief in half at corners.

2. Fold corners #2 and #3 into the center.

3. Roll from the bottom up to corner #1.

4. Fold the roll into thirds.

5. While holding the roll and keeping points together, fold points back away from folded thirds, wrapping them around the roll. Continue tucking the layers under.

6. Keep wrapping the layers under until #2 & #3 come back out as tails.

7. Fold the point of one of the tails back over body and pin to form the head of the mouse.

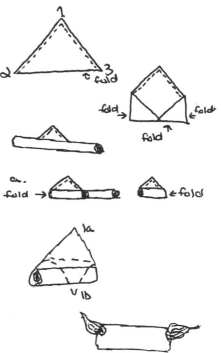

I noticed on leaving that the young mother had planted new cabbage plants around the the small fruit trees, using even that small space both to grow food and be pleasing to the eye.

Children all have responsibilities in the homes. Large families are a way of life for many reasons. Children are their joy and families are large, because many hands working together make the work load lighter. Also families are their community, church and social life. From a very early age, chores are given to children. On visiting a family one fall day, I observed a nine-year-old boy and seven-year-old girl cleaning out gutters in the barn. They had a wheelbarrow by the door and were pitching manure into it. They came running up to where I stood with feet bare, the boy's trousers smothered with manure and the girl's little burgundy dress front covered with spatterings. Both were all smiles. We visited and I showed them my movable wind-up Halloween pins. After this brief visit, they resumed their chores.

One nine-year-old boy had the responsibility of cleaning the pig house three times weekly. Shredded paper was used in the pens for bedding. He also filled large barrels with feed using a wagon he pulled behind him. He'd place the two buckets into the wagon, fill them and then go empty them into the barrels until they were full. Two smaller children followed him to and from the pig pens observing and keeping him company. On the return to fill the buckets, the two-year-old was placed in the bucket with only her head showing. It took many trips.

I was surprised to hear one Amish woman say that her seven- and nine-year-old nieces were her legs. They would come over and do errands such as going to the basement, up the stairs, or to the garden or into the larder. When there is an invalid in the homes, these little ones learn young to be the legs, saving adults for the larger chores. Great lessons are learned in caring and being compassionate in nature.

When newborns join a family, little nieces, sisters or a hired older girl help out. One little girl thought she should rest whenever the new mother did... and that wasn't what she was there for.

Boys and girls do chicken, pig, and milking chores and help with field work. Since milking is done by hand, many hands make light work. I was told that gravel is not to be spread in driveways nor is lime spread in the fields by truck because those are things of our world. The gravel is put to the side of the road. One Amish grandparent told me, "It gives the young ones something to do. They load it into a wheelbarrow or wagon and fill potholes."

Even though there are many chores for both boys and girls, there is also time for fun. One family, after the small chickens had been moved out of a newly built chicken house, cleaned it out and made it into a playhouse furnished with a table with an oil cloth over it. An older brother made a free-standing cabinet (hutch) for dishes; a small hickory rocker was placed inside and two small chairs at the table. At the windows were dark navy blue curtains, hung with a string.

Young girls have a poise beyond their years and boys and girls appear to be young adults, miniature men and women. They mature swiftly because they are treated as adults at a very young age, given responsibilities and spoken to in a matter-of-fact manner, as parents might speak to each other. Since visiting is a major part of their lifestyle and is the source of entertainment, without the interference of TV, radio, Nintendo, and other electronic devices, I believe the communication between family members is great. Children have a sense of security and belonging. Early on, they are a part of the family where humor, teasing, family fun and being helpful are communicated. They don't have to wonder what life jobs or work-related lifestyles will be. They know that, by being a part of a larger family-oriented community, caring, sharing and jobs will be there—Amish-related jobs of course. Women, become wives, mothers, teachers or midwives, take up wood crafts (one makes cedar chests), make quilts, do basket weaving, and are caretakers (going from home to home as hired girls giving home and health care). Experience and learning from their elders is their guidance and training.

Two Amish boys from different families, ages 14 and 16, have a stature that radiates self-assurance, security, and a sense of well being. They are, in some ways, men in boy's bodies. The younger of the two made small crude wood crafts at age 10 and by age 14 makes furniture pieces that most adults would take pride in. The older has been out of school for two or three years (since the eighth grade). He helps other Amish farmers in the area, as does the younger boy, and has begun to learn a trade in woodcrafts. The older boy began by helping his father, who makes windows, cabinets, and other items. The son found a pattern for toys and began enjoying this small venture, making big-wheel trucks, trailers, tractors, scoops and a one-pronged haylift for it. He sold these at a local country store in Henrytown to our Englishers. While working in the shop he was asked what he did for fun, and very simply answered, "This."

Amish children are disciplined in a very matter-of-fact way. Forms of discipline range from spanking to verbal correction, etc. It is taken for granted that they are to share in the responsibility of caring for home, farm, and family. Children learn by observing and doing. The security of belonging to a family is learned through daily association in work, play, and the leisure of a visiting Sunday. These are learned through the church community, and anything that brings the family together. At a very young age they learn a sense of accomplishment, and responsibility, and they know that they, too, are helping the family. A three- and six-year-old may gather eggs and collect wood for Mama's woodburning stove. Older children help with child care, baking, washing clothes, gardening, canning, etc. They are taught to respect their elders. When I visit Amish homes the children are actively participating in the household chores. They may quietly congregate around the adults or go about their chores as usual.

If you think Amish children don't have fun, think again. With their horse and buggy, they go to visit with other families where there are always children to play with. They use their imaginations as there aren't plentiful toys.

 They play Annie-I-Over, tag, baseball, hide-and-seek, board games such as checkers; they have swings with wooden seats, and playhouses; they go fishing, hunting, ice skating, sledding, playing in the snow, building forts and snowmen, making hideouts out of bales in the hay mow; indoors they work with crayons, clay, paints, paper crafts, basket making, and any number of things. Most activities are family- and community-oriented.

A typical day in the life of an Amish child, from what I have observed and been told, goes something like this: The family arises at the crack of dawn, usually around 5 a.m. Standard time is always observed; they do not change to Daylight Saving Time. Boys get up, put chore clothes on and start for the barn with their father while the girls get up, assist with the smaller children, help pack school lunches (during school time) and help prepare for breakfast by setting the table and sweeping the floors. The mother is busy directing and assisting with these many chores. The woodburning stove is fired for warmth in the colder months and when it is hot enough breakfast preparation can be done. Scrambled eggs, fried potatoes, side pork, bread, butter, jam, and a bowl of fruit are typical dishes served at large breakfasts.

In the barn, the boys and their father have begun feeding the cows and washing them in preparation for milking by hand. Each boy will milk about two cows. The mother often goes to the barn to help with the milking. The girls have been set in motion with their chores and the mother will return when she is through with the milking. While the young men wash up, mother and the girls place the bowls and plates of food on the table and get the little ones into highchairs and up to the table. Everyone is seated at the long harvest table on backless benches. The family bows their heads in silent prayer. There is much participation in conversation at the table. After the meal, the young boys and the father are back in the barn for calf chores and cleaning the gutters.

46

During the spring, gophers begin to dig in the fields. Trapping begins and these traps need to be checked morning and night. The county pays a small price for the gopher feet to encourage this trapping. One of the boys will go check the traps and reset them while the other boys finish the barn chores. The girls, after helping to clear away the breakfast dishes, go upstairs and dress for school. On returning to the kitchen, they wash and put the dishes away. One girl sits at the table picking walnut meat out of the nuts her mother has cracked for her. The mother may eventually go and stitch at the quilt frame in front of the window while the smaller children play on the floor. The baby is sitting in the small crib beside her, playing with large beads on a string. The boys are soon finished with their chores, and wash up and change their clothing for school. The girls and boys, with coats on, lunch buckets in hand, and school books under their arms, walk down the road on their way to school.

This whole process will begin again 1 to 1 1/2 hours after returning from school about 3:30 p.m. Before the evening chores begin, the children will have a snack, visit and play. One family near us has boys who trap gophers on the field in front of our farm home. These boys check their traps on their way to and from school. Their sisters and smaller brothers continue walking down the country road and soon the boys catch up after checking and resetting the traps.

In the evening after their meal the children and parents relax, visit, read, sew, and play. Bedtime is between 8 and 9 p.m.

One little boy I know got up at the usual time one morning and helped his dad with the milking chores and helped set out the milk cans for the milk truck. Then he ate breakfast, and with his brother (the boys were 8 and 10 years old) went to visit their aunt who had just had a new baby. They walked down an old road that used to be for horses and buggies but is now unused. It winds through a field and across a bridge. The trip to and from the aunt's house was about a mile. The boys were back at their own house by 8:00 a.m. and were going out to do the rabbit chores — feeding and watering the rabbits. Then they changed out of their chore jackets into their school jackets and hats and walked to school — another 1/4 mile. All of this happened between about 5:30 a.m. and 8:45 a.m!

Teachers give their children composition books to write poetry and draw pictures. Note there are no names or pictures of people in the following poem and drawings (graven images-Deuteronomy 5:8-10)

Helping my Neighbor

Our neighbor came to us one day,
And asked, "Could I have one to make hay."
It won't be till next Monday,
'Cause I only started mowing today.

Dad said, "Yes, I guess you can."
And on Monday noon over to the neighbor I ran,
When I came over he was raking hay.
When he saw me he said, "Nice day."

He said he would make one more round,
'Till I get the grease gun found.
It should be somewhere in the shop,
Maybe on the wood-bench top.

Next we started making a load.
It was in that field beside the road.
I drove the team and helped load hay
And soon we had all the hay away.

This poem had the name of the farmer ("our neighbor") and the name of the hired helper ("one"). Names were removed because Amish do not call attention to themselves (pride is considered a sin).

A PaPer Plate makes
a fine spaceship

This picture was drawn by a 4th grader with some knowledge of the world.

One Of Nature's Many Scenes!

This picture was drawn by an 11 year old in grade 5. Note steel wheels on machinery.

This picture was drawn by a 6th grade boy with a sense of humor. It's a dog fishing?

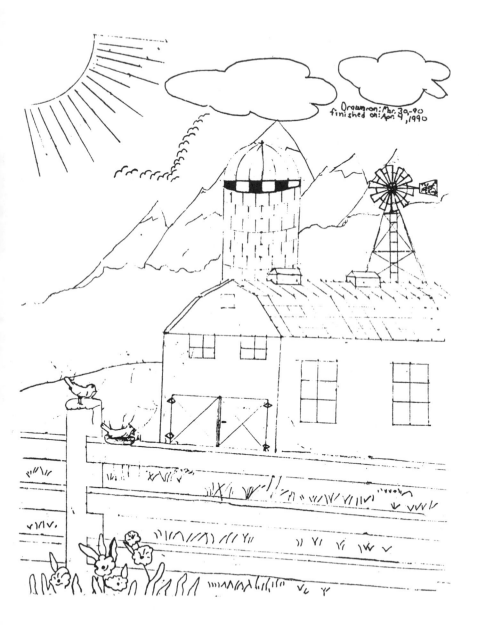

This picture was drawn by a 13 year old in 7th grade.

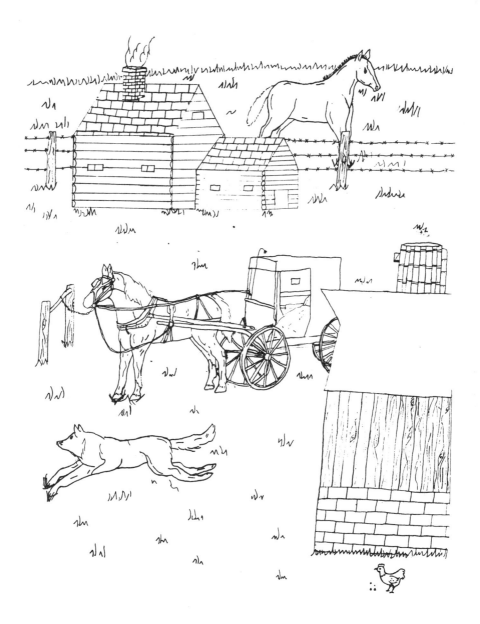

This picture was drawn by a 12 year old in grade 7.

53

This picture was done by a 14 year old in grade 8. "Wild Horses on a high cliff And a Western Sunset."

This picture was drawn by an eighth grade boy. Note the broken fence. "It looks as if it would be time to fix fence."

Children's Remedies and Recipes

I have collected some recipes for children and include them here. Some are remedies for common childhood ailments, some for common childhood predicaments, and some are recipes that children simply enjoy.

A six-year-old Amish boy with blond hair and blue eyes ran up to the car. "My brother's in trouble!" I asked why. He replied, "Because he painted my boots white and our little dog white, too." The evidence of this dilemma greeted us as we rounded the corner of the house. Mother was outside at work trying to wash out the three-year-old's paint-spattered pants. The little black dog, now white, lay dejectedly under the porch. When I entered the house, I saw a three-year-old sitting on the day bed with traces of tears on his face. I suggested she use the following recipe to remove paint from the boy and the dog:

To remove paint: Use butter or lard. This is very good for getting paint off sensitive skin areas such as the face.

For loose bowels: Take 1 cup of raw oatmeal and 3 cups of water. Let soak several minutes. Pour off water and give it to child. If bottle-fed, give instead of milk.

For diaper rash or exzema: Rub oatmeal paste on area after cleansing with warm water.

To prevent diaper rash: Pat or dust dry cornstarch on rash area.

For fever: Bathe skin with cool water with a small amount of alcohol to bring fever down. Cold cloths and towels can be laid over the body and changed as often as they become warm if fever is very high.

When a child had a fever and woke in the middle of the night, his mother took two bread sacks and cut raw onions into both, put bags over the child's bare feet and tied them on. In the morning, the onions were mushy. The mother claimed the fever had been drawn out into the onions.

For tangles in hair: A little vinegar in water as a rinse helps remove soap residue and softens hair.

For colic: Put 1 drop of peppermint in 2 ounces of water. Or put 3 drops of liquid herbal and fennel extract in 1 ounce of water, or have druggist mix 1 ounce glycerin, 10 drops aconite tincture and 1 ounce of water. Give 2 to 5 drops of this mixture twice a day for three days. Wait three days and repeat.

For teething children: Rub Vicks ointment on sore gums.

Cure for a child who stands up in a highchair: Tie shoelaces together.

For a child sliding down in a highchair: Place a rolling pin between spokes and under legs.

For a fussy child: Make catnip tea and bottle feed.

For a child with constipation: Make slippery elm tea,[4] 1 tsp. per cup. Boil 10 to 20 minutes. Add more water if it gets too thick.

Note to the reader: I do not recommend the use of these remedies and suggest you seek the advice of a physician for all conditions and diseases.

Animal crackers

2 cups sugar	2 eggs
1 cup butter	3-4 cups of flour
1 cup milk	3 tsp. baking powder
1 or 2 drops of lemon flavor	

Cream sugar and butter together adding eggs one at a time, beating well after each. Add milk alternately with flour. In first cup of flour add 3 tsp. baking powder. Add flour until very stiff dough is formed. Roll thin like a pie crust and cut into animal shapes.

Lolly Pops

When making white bread, make several small pops (balls) and place in a greased pan. Let it rise to double its size. After it has risen, mix 1/2 or more cups of cream and 1/4 cup white or brown sugar and pour over pops just before baking. Bake at 350° for 15 minutes or until brown. Eat while warm.

Play Dough

Mix and set aside: •1 cup flour •1/2 cup salt •1 tbs alum

Put in pan: •1 cup water •1 tbs oil •food coloring •peppermint flavoring

Stir flour mixture into liquid and place over medium heat, stirring constantly until thickened. Remove form heat and place on wax paper to cool. Keep in a covered container in a cool place. The peppermint drops add a nice aroma.

Clay

Combine 3 cups of flour, 1 cup of salt and 1/3 cup oil. Add enough cold water to make it the consistency of dough.

---

[4] Old fashioned ingredients can be obtained by writing to Clark's Natural Herbs, P.O. Box 12, Chaffee, New York 14030.

Old Order Amish Schools

There are six one-room Amish schools in the Harmony-Canton area:
1. Star Corner School — Amherst Township
2. Grub School — Canton Township
3. Vail School — Canton Township
4. Wilton Center School — Harmony Township
5. Valley View School — Canton Township
6. Scotland School — Preston Township

These schools are placed within a reasonable radius, making them accessible to Amish farms. Advanced education is not valued in their culture. Specifically, their education consists of an eighth grade elementary education. (Some students on completion of eighth grade are as young as 13 or 14 years of age.) An apprenticiship, to learn a trade, is often times a form of ongoing education. They believe common sense is more important than knowledge. They speak low German (called Pennsylvania Dutch) in their homes. Little children who are under school age understand only German; English is taught after entering school at the age of six. On Fridays all of the lessons are taught in German.

Star Corner School—Amherst Township

The Grub School (originally the old Vail schoolhouse) has a woodshed attached. Note outdoor toilets behind school.

Valley View School

The Amish call this old store the Vail School.

The Wilton Center School is the largest Amish school, with approximately 45 students and two teachers in 1993.

The Scotland School

Schools teach the four "R's" (Reading, 'Riting, 'Rithmetic, and Respect). They believe in a life of goodness and self-denial, fostering the teachings of the Bible from dawn until dusk in the way they relate to one another.

Teachers have no formal education and are not state certified, Amish teachers are eighth grade educated and are what they term "easy learners," (good students). Teachers may have been "teacher's helpers" at one time. Often times an experienced teacher will help train a new teacher and assist her until she is comfortable with the schedule, material, and students. Teachers have been as young as sixteen but generally are older. Remembering conversations involving the schools brings to mind this story:

The Amish school board had visited the family of a potential school teacher. After they had left, the shy young girl who was being considered made this statement: "It wouldn't do for me to teach from under the desk." Even though she was shy, she did teach for several years.

Schools have had from as few as seventeen scholars to as many as forty. The largest school has had two teachers. They were half sisters through marriage, with only one year's difference in age and the same birth date.

It is easy to understand why "school board and parents support their teachers," especially when teachers often teach their younger brothers and sisters, nieces and nephews. The Amish school year often ends sooner than our public school. Why? Because they don't take the vacation breaks our public schools do. They do celebrate the Christian holidays but not with extended vacations. Their school breaks are taken out of necessity (for sickness, funerals, church, community or school district functions.) Schools do not start their opening day at the same time nor end their school year at the same time. (One school had a late start because of school repairs and painting.) Saturday is used as an extra school day whenever days need to be made up; otherwise Monday through Friday are the usual days attended.

They pay taxes, including our school tax levies (although they take no state aid) and follow these state requirements concerning education: 1)They keep attendance records, 2)Students attend the required number of school days (170), 3)They attend the required hours for a school day, 4)Schools teach the basics, 5)Teachers follow health and safety standards (but immunizations are not required.).

These are stick teepees in the Scotland school yard. The children put them together, playing, and later used them for kindling in the woodburning stoves.

On any given day in fall, winter, or springtime I have observed many groups of Amish children arriving at school carrying black metal lunch buckets, dressed in dark colors, and wearing straw hats and bonnets.

The children play softball in a field close by or in the school yard. In warmer weather, straw hats and jackets can be seen hanging on fence posts. Games like Annie-I-Over are played throwing a ball over the school house. Children at one school built teepees out of sticks around trees. In the winter, sleds can be observed lined up along fences or leaning against the school. Snow forts are a common sight.

In the school houses woodburning stoves are started by the closest Amish neighbor or the teacher. Large bulletin boards are used to display crafts, grades, and improvements (by the star system, using gold, silver, red and blue.) Large slate blackboards are used for teaching.

The Grammar in Rhyme

A noun is a name of anything,
    As school or garden, hoop or ring.
Adjectives tell what kind of noun,
    Great, small, pretty, white, or brown.
Instead of a noun a pronoun stands,
    For John's head, his face, my hand.
Verbs tell of something being done,
    To read, write, sing, spell, or run.
Before the noun a preposition stands,
    To the church, from a tree, on his land.
"I connect" The conjunction says,
    Sentences and words, tomorrow or today.
How things are done the adverb tells,
    As slowly, quickly, ill, or well.
They also tell us where and when,
    As here, there, now, and then.
Interjections show surprise,
    As "Oh" how pretty and "Oh" how wise.

Most of the teaching materials for the Amish schools come from Ontario, Canada, or Ohio. They also use our old readers, which were used during the 1930s and 1940s, and there is a magazine printed to serve as a teacher's guide (called "The Blackboard Bulletin") that is available for their use.

An example of readers used is Our Heritage which is part of the Pathway Reading Series, published by Pathway Publishing Corp. of Aylmer, Ontario and LaGrange, Indiana. Titles of other books in the series are Thinking of Others — Fifth grade; Step by Step — Sixth grade; and Seeking True Values — Seventh grade. Our Heritage is the Eighth grade textbook. Editors of the series are Joseph Stoll, David Luthy, and Elmo Stoll. In Our Heritage contents are:

Unit One — Our Heritage
Unit Two — True Values
Unit Three — People Who Served
Unit Four — Thinking of Others
Unit Five — Nature's Wonders
Unit Six — In Olden Days
Unit Seven — The Way of Love
Unit Eight — Home on the Farm

Each unit begins with a Bible verse. For example Unit One's Bible verse is Psalms 61:5. . . "Thou hast given me the heritage of those that fear thy name." On the following page is the poem, Our Help in Ages Past by Isaac Watts:

"O God, our help is ages past,
Our hope for years to come,
Our shelter from the stormy blast
And our eternal home. . . "
(there are eight verses)

The story, "Church in the Pasture" follows the poem. Preface to story: "Because of persecution, our Anabaptist forefathers often met at night for religious services — in fields or barns or in the deep forest. The following story is about such a meeting which occurred 'in a field just outside Leeuwarden (The Netherlands) in 1542.' It is an adaptation of chapter 13 of the book The Drummer's Wife. "One of the speakers at this nighttime meeting was Menno Simons, whose biography 'One Hundred Guilders for Menno' you will find in a later unit of this book."

The story is followed by Thinking-It-Over questions and Word Study: tremble, amble, reverberate, lot, alien, conspire, asunder, villain, traitor.

After eighth grade education ends, their learning process goes on. Amish never go on to vocational schools or college. A trade is learned by "hands-on experience" called apprenticeship. Young people train to be farmers, harness craftsmen, builders of buggies, wheelwrights, blacksmiths, carpenters, furniture craftsmen, midwives, caretakers, etc.

One craftsman and grandfather had his grandsons about, helping and observing in his shop, keeping him company and learning his trade from his experience, patience and good humor. I once went into his furniture craftshop to order what I called at that time a youth chair. (It is a highchair without arms.) He corrected me saying, "It is a mamachair." I asked, "Why do you call it a mamachair?" He replied, "Because mama sits on it to get off her feet." I said, "It's awfully small," to which he replied with a gleam in his eye and a smile on his face, "Yes, and mama is all sizes, but the chair stays the same size."

A small child's hutch made by a young Amish Boy.

Toys made for Englishers but not for Amish children.

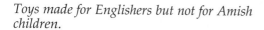

Secrets

Courtship

The secrets among the Amish are not really secrets at all, yet what fun they have concerning courtship, weddings, and babies. Like a game being played, a great deal of fun and humor revolve around these events. No one is supposed to know who is courting whom but it's like our gossip; news travels fast, and soon everyone knows.

I remember one particular night. My husband and I were on our way home after eating out. The hour was about 9:30 or 10 pm. Traveling home on the gravel roads towards our farm, we noticed a buggy in the ditch. The night was dark, since the moon was not large. The buggy, being black, was almost invisible to us. He appeared to be hiding from us. I said to my husband, "Do you see a buggy? He thinks we can't see him." Most likely, it was a young Amish man and woman courting.

Another time many years ago I awoke very early one summer morning. Our bedroom windows were open. It was a quiet morning and I could hear the sound of buggy wheels on the gravel road (sound travels well on still days). I looked at our nightstand clock; the hour was 3:50 am. I felt sure one of the Amish neighbor boys was just coming home from courting.

Courtship (or "dating" as I was corrected by one young Amish man) takes place in the home where young people, beginning at the age of 17, have get-togethers. They do not go to the movies or to town for entertainment. They call these gatherings "singings." These are held every two weeks. They sing for one to one and a half hours. Lunch is served later in the evening (popcorn, cookies, or half moon pies with coffee or a cold drink) , The boys at times can be full of horseplay that is rough and boisterous, but this is outside and away from the girls. Teasing, humor, conversation, food, and eye contact are all a part of courtship. Boys and girls may pair up for these gatherings.

"Bundling" is a form of courtship among the Amish and is allowed after there is a commitment of probable marriage. Bundling is accepted because families are large and there is very little privacy, and for practical reasons such as distance. Bundling is "an ancient courtship custom of northern Europe and the British Isles, transported to England by the early settlers. In bundling, engaged couples, either partly or fully clothed, lie in the same bed, sometimes with a special board between them. Frequently it was the only time lovers were permitted to be alone together. The custom may have had its origins as a means of saving fuel, since only the main room of the house was heated. After much notoriety, bundling disappeared in the United States in the early 19th century."[5] The same rules for courting are recommended as in days of old. A state of purity is to be upheld; if not, the couple must confess publicly.

Once I asked a young Amish man how long it took to go twenty miles by horse and buggy. He replied, "It takes one hour to go twenty miles." When this was asked of an older Amish man he said, "It takes longer than that! An hour and half is more likely the time it takes." I replied laughing, "maybe he was on his way to his girlfriend's and ran the horse." I asked another young married man, "When you were courting did you ever race your horses?" He laughed and replied, "No, I just tried to stay ahead."

There are a number of occasions which allow relationships to develop. No doubt some are as imaginative as the following story.

A widowed Amish man had a hired man. The hired man wrote to a lady who had lost her husband and he signed the widowed man's name! This began a correspondence that led to eventual marriage.

I have been asked several times about intermarriage among the Amish. They do allow second-cousin marriages. One lady in the community, with help, has put together a genealogy book which is very large, to keep track of family relationships.

Young people visit relatives in other states and communities which may lead to relationships outside of the community and new blood lines. Also, young girls sometimes work in other communities, thereby fostering new relationships.

Weddings

Weddings are kept a secret until two weeks before the ceremony. October through March are the usual marrying months since weddings are planned so that they don't interfere with the planting and harvest seasons. They are usually on a Tuesday or Thursday, therefore not interfering with the church Sundays.

I have had some personal experience with the secrecy surrounding weddings. I was visiting Amish friends three weeks

---

[5] *Grolier's Universal Encyclopedia.* NY, Grolier Incorporated, 1965. Vol. 3, pg 94.

before their daughter was to be married. (This was unknown to me, however.) It was a day of sewing for them. They offered me a chair and continued piecing and sewing their garments. They were probably sewing for the wedding. While we visited, one daughter sat at a treadle sewing machine stitching a garment. We visited as they continued their work. I laughingly related the following story and conversation:

I had been shopping at the grocery store in Harmony and mistook an Amish man for his younger brother. I was a bit embarrassed, as I'd never met this man before. Trying to cover my embarrassment I said, "You boys certainly look alike." Still embarrassed and trying to make conversation, I remarked, "I've heard your brother moved onto a farm not far from your father. He must be getting married." He laughingly said, "He is?" I asked, "Doesn't he have a girlfriend in Ohio?" He replied still smiling, "He does?" Of course, courtship and marriage being a secret, he wasn't going to divulge anything. My Amish friends later explained this concept to me.

A week or so went by and I returned to the same Amish home. On this visit I was told of the upcoming marriage of their daughter because it had been published (announced) in church by the bishop. "Publishing" is the announcement of marriage two weeks before the upcoming marriage. The secret then becomes public knowledge. I then realized that they, too, had never divulged their daughter's upcoming marriage and were aware of their own "secret" even as I related my encounter at the grocery store.

In April of the following year, I was visiting two Amish friends (one of whom was the sister of the two brothers in the earlier story.) I told her of my conversation with her brother almost a year before. She, too, had a big laugh on me. She said, "I've got a secret to tell you." I asked, "What's this about now?" I just knew something was tickling her. She told me, her eyes twinkling in laughter, "My brother is getting married!" The wedding was in Ohio.

Marriages are not prearranged by parents choosing spouses for their children. Amish choose their own mates and are usually young adults of twenty years old or more when they marry. Young people are given time for "running around," considered a time of growing up and decision making. More choices and freedom are allowed before they are baptised and make a real commitment to Amish life. Baptism is encouraged at about the age of eighteen. A young man may "put off" baptism until he decides to marry, but baptism is necessary before marriage. There is no divorce in Old Order Amish communities.

After the marriage is"published" or announced in one of the "church homes", the hustle and bustle of preparations begin. Invitations are by word of mouth, but are mailed to distant friends and relatives. Very few Englishers are invited. "Side-sitters" (attendants) are chosen. They are called side-sitters because they sit beside the bride and groom. They are single young people, and their identities are also kept secret.

Clothing for the wedding is sewn. The groom's family makes him a long cape-like overcoat with hook and eye closures, a white shirt with no collar or lapels, (using two buttons at the neck), a black jacket and pants of gabardine or worsted wool. The bride makes her own dress and can choose one of the dark colors for her wedding. She will wear a black prayer kapp the day of her wedding and thereafter will wear a white lawn prayer kapp. A long white lawn apron will be worn over her dark dress.

The church benches are set up in the main room and the adjoining rooms. Two homes are prepared, one where the wedding will be held and one (one of the parents' homes) where the reception is held. That way food preparation can be made and tables set up ahead of time. Sheet cakes are made, and are frosted but not decorated. Sometimes a star-shaped cake (the bridal cake) is cut from a sheet cake. Chicken, dressing, potatoes, gravy, vegetables, jello, and cakes are the usual fare.

A visiting Bishop is sometimes asked ahead of time to perform the wedding service. It is considered a courtesy. When guests have arrived and are seated the ceremony begins. It will last approximately four hours. The men sit in the main room; young unmarried men & women sit separately in the kitchen. Only a few married women attend because they are preparing for the reception in a home nearby. Mothers of the couple being married go to the wedding to hear the vows of marriage, returning to the food preparation shortly after.

The bride and groom wait in an upstairs bedroom apart from where the guests have gathered. When guests have arrived, the Bishop and ministers proceed down the stairs after the young couple. There is no music, only silence as they enter. The side-sitters (attendants) wait in the kitchen. When the bride and groom arrive downstairs, side-sitters, who have been a "secret" up until this time, then join them in the center of the main room. The

Bishop takes his place in a doorway between the two rooms (both are filled) so he can be heard by all the guests. The side-sitters and the bride and groom sit facing each other in the center of the main room. The service begins with singing which one man leads. There are no musical instruments. The Bishop begins with a prayer, followed by a long sermon of about forty-five minutes, and a short sermon of about thirty minutes. Vows are spoken, answered by "yah, yah" and a curtsy from the bride and groom. Then there are Bible readings. The ceremony including the sermon is performed in German. There is no kissing or hugging, but there is handholding. Rings are not exchanged and there is no honeymoon (unless visiting relatives is considered a honeymoon). During the service when the congregation sits the bride and groom stand.

After the ceremony there is much visiting but no congratulations. Everyone goes to his or her own horse and buggy to proceed to the parents' house for the celebration of the wedding. Tables are set up in a "U"-shape lining the walls. (All the furniture in the house has been removed). The bride, groom and side-sitters sit at a special corner table called the "Eck." The bishops, ministers, and deacons sit at another table. A silent prayer is observed before the food is served. After the meal fruit or candybars are sometimes given to guests plus cigars to the men. Many guests stay late into the evening to help with cleaning up. In the evening the young single boys and girls have a "singing," visiting and having fun. A simple meal is served near evening, and by late evening or early morning everyone has departed for home.

The young married couple spends the first night at the home of one of the parents. The bride, groom and side-sitters do all the dishes the following day. I heard it said in a joking manner, "We do the work preparing for the wedding. They can do the dishes." The young people have fun while doing the dishwashing, talking over the previous day's events, laughing and joking.

The couple may rent, build, move a house onto the parents' building site or live with parents until a place can be found for them. This varies from family to family.

On one occasion on the day following the wedding I was shown the wedding gifts. In an upstairs bedroom the groom's family was writing down the names and the gifts given in a notebook. Downstairs the bride, groom, and side-sitters were doing the dishes. Gifts were practical—Tools, glass items, pots, pans, battery operated flashlights, canned goods, linens, rugs, and

71

colored glassware, but nothing elaborate. Parents' gifts to children vary greatly from livestock and fowl to furniture, money, linens, silverware, etc.

The following recipe was given to me by a young married Amish girl. It was her wedding cake. A corner cake is a wedding cake and a family favorite. It is given this name because the wedding couple and their side-sitters sit at the corner of tables arranged in a "U"-shape.

A Corner Cake

1 1/2 cups white sugar	1/2 cup sweet milk
1/2 cup boiling water	1/2 teasp. salt
1/2 cup lard or margarine	3 egg whites beaten stiff
3 cups flour	1/2 cup nuts if desired
3 teasp. baking powder	

Grease and flour a 9 X 13 pan. Mix sugar and shortening; add boiling water. Sift flour, baking powder, and salt together. Add dry ingredients alternately with milk. Fold in egg whites last. Bake thirty to forty minutes at 350°F.

One young married Amish girl asked, "Do you know how love starts?" She answered, "With an 'L'."

Birthing and Midwives

The stories I will relate regarding birthing and midwives are humorous and considerate of Amish beliefs and sensitivities.

To begin with, it must be understood that in the Amish community nothing sexual is mentioned in front of children. It reminds me of stories I've heard older women of our English-speaking world relate. To say the least, it was a closed subject.

One spring day, a friend and I went visiting a young Amish mother with two boys. They were playing in a room close by. She called my friend and me away from her four- and six-year-old boys to the entry of the house. Closing the door behind her, she whispered, "I have a secret to tell you. We're going to have a baby." Truthfully, it was very obvious, and it was no secret! However it was a joy to see her anticipation and excitement at the prospect of another child in the home.

A few weeks later, I stopped by again. We visited and before leaving, I quietly stepped to her calendar (one of the few things on the walls of Amish homes) and, pointing to a date on it, I said, "My daughter is here. Where are you?" She stepped to the calendar and quietly pointed to a date. That summer I had a new grandson and she had a baby girl.

I also recall a time when something similar took place. I unintentionally stopped by at meal time. ("They" stay on standard time when "we" go on daylight saving time.) I apologized and said I'd come back later. I was assured it was okay and urged to stay. Mother was bustling about in the kitchen, as the others were finishing their meal. The father and the five children, a little girl in a high chair, an older sister, and three boys sat eating at a long harvest table. While visiting, I inquired about the new baby in her brother's family. "I understand your brother has helped with the delivery of several of his children. Is that true?" The mother hesitated, looking from me to the children around the table, and then at her husband. Turning back to me, she replied, "We do talk about that sometimes." I understood immediately; it was a subject not talked about in front of children.

There are women in the Amish community—mothers, aunts, and grandmothers—who have learned birthing procedures and remedies from others who have preceded them. They do not publicly claim to be midwives. Women of their own Amish community send for them, knowing they will oversee and coach the birthing process, giving comfort and support. Amish women visit doctors for prenatal care, and most first-born children are born in hospitals.

One fall day I received a phone call from a neighbor who lived close to the Amish. I was asked if I would go and pick up a midwife. I also picked up the young father's mother, who would assist. The midwife brought with her a rather large black bag. I drove down a long, steep, tree-lined driveway to the home, let the two women out, and turned my car around to leave. As I drove back up the driveway, I observed the midwife and her assistant pasted against the wash house wall, out of sight. I proceeded up the hill, looking back on the opposite side of the house, and I saw the children being hurried out the back door and across the field to auntie's house. It was a "secret" and later a surprise in the form of a new brother or sister.

I was told by midwives that it is God's hand that is at work in all things. To boast of their own good deeds is to give God dishonor.

These are two recipes given to me by midwives:

Parturient Balm — a soothing remedy to induce and promote labor.

> 4 oz. blue cahosh root*
> 1 oz. lady slipper root*
> 1 oz. spikenard root*
> 1/2 oz. sassafrass*
> 1/2 oz. clove (whole)*

Simmer slowly for two hours in two quarts of boiling water. Strain and add one pound of white sugar or honey. Take two to four tablespoons twice daily, for four or five weeks previous to due date. Dry tea shavings and use again.

Angelica Root Tea — Good for loosening the afterbirth.

It is a herb also called archangel. Put one teaspoon tea in one cup of boiling water and steep. Stir and allow to cool. Strain. Drink one or two cups daily for two to four weeks before delivery.

---

* Herbs can be bought through catalogs from people who specialize in obtaining botanicals from fields and forests, cut and sifted for tea use.

Church In The Homes

There are five church districts in this Amish community. One of the five church districts split off from the larger church district because of the slow-moving vehicle laws in Minnesota.* When two districts have a "church Sunday" the other two districts have a "visiting Sunday."

Church is every second Sunday and families take turns rotating this event from home to home. Before a church Sunday, a thorough cleaning is done. Collapsible benches (called church benches) are brought to the home where services will be held. They will be set up on two walls  opposite each other, leaving the center of the room open. Men and boys will sit on one side and women and smaller children on the other side. The Bishop or Minister stands on one end in the center aisle. A room is provided for mothers if babies become fussy. Church services last approximately three hours, beginning at about 9 a.m. and lasting until noon.

There is a song leader in each church. Deacons read Bible scripture and Ministers or Bishops preach. All services are in High German. Bibles are Luther's translation and are written in German. Sometimes there is a meeting after church services to discuss community matters. Everyone stays for the noon meal, which consists of bean soup. This soup is served every Sunday.

Bean Soup

1/2 lb. soup beans (navy)	3 qts. milk
3 1/2 tsp. salt	4 or 5 Tbs butter

Wash and cook beans until soft. Drain water off. Set aside. Melt and brown the butter. Add the beans and mix well. Add the milk, stirring occasionally. Bring to a boil. Add salt. Cut stale dried or toasted bread into very thin pieces and add to soup, to the thickness you prefer.

---

* See chapter titled, Government and State Law

Church is held in homes because during the Protestant Reformation the Anabaptists were persecuted by both the Church of Rome and the reformers. This made it necessary for them to move about and keep their worship secretive.* In order to survive, religious services were held in fields, barns, or in deep forests. Therefore they still do not have services in a formal church building. It is a carryover from days gone by.

On a church Sunday many buggies are seen on the gravel roads all traveling in the same general direction; large family buggies as well as smaller buggies. Women wear white aprons over dark dresses and white prayer kapps and young single girls are in dark pleated prayer kapps. Both have large black bonnets over their kapps. Boys and men wear white shirts and dark pants. Church Sunday is a day of both worship and relaxation. In fact, all the church holidays are observed as a day of reverence as well as a day of rest.

Each two church districts have a Bishop and a Deacon. Each individual district has at least two Ministers. Bishops, Ministers and Deacons are called to their vocation by Holy Spirit or by divine appointment (Acts 1:24-26). Their appointment is ratified by the church and acknowledged by laying on of hands by elders (Acts 6:6), an ancient practice of ordination.

Leaders are chosen by casting lots and one who is so chosen cannot refuse leadership. (Proverbs 16:33: "The lot is cast into the lap, but the decision is wholly from the Lord.") Casting lots was common from the days of Moses to that of David but afterwards it fell into disuse. It had religious associations and was an unusual way of settling questions, such as dividing land, inheritance and other difficult matters (Jos 18:6-28; Mt 27:35). To choose lots, the congregation visits and gives their input as to who is a man of good faith, and a good family man. (1 Timothy 3:1-2 and 1 Timothy 3:8-13). Sometimes an open window is used for casting lots. (Different methods can be used to cast lots.) Each baptised member of the congregation quietly goes to this window and speaks a name to someone outside. Whoever receives two marks or more is in the lot. Using only these names, then, each member again speaks a name. Whoever is chosen is therefore believed to be led by the spirit of God to be a leader of his flock.

In order to be chosen Bishop, a man must have been a minister, which puts him in a mature age bracket..

* See chapter titled, *Old Order Amish Schools,* Preface to the story, *"Church in the Pasture."*

76

The Bishops' functions include leadership, preaching God's word, preserving God's people from error, and watching or caring for the flock. The Deacons' functions include Bible reading, caring for the poor and taking care of temporal affairs.

Public confessions are encouraged. James 5:16 says, "Therefore confess your sins to one another and pray for one another that you may be healed, the prayer of a righteous man has great power in its effects." Also see Romans 10:9 and Psalms 32:5.

In addition to weddings (described in another chapter), the other special occasions that take place during a church year are described below.

Communion

Communion is held two times a year, in the spring and fall. The elements are homemade bread and homemade wine. A common cup is used. Ministers and Bishops have a helper to serve communion. After partaking of bread and wine, footwashing begins, a sign of true humility. It symbolizes washing and purification of the soul in the blood of Christ.[6] Men wash men's feet and women wash women's feet, proceeding two by two, in pairs of four until all have taken part. Partners are not chosen in any particular order or beforehand. Singing is done throughout these services.

Baptism

Baptism is a time for adults (usually a person is eighteen years and older) to commit their lives to God. Instructions in preparation for baptism are given by the Bishop for nine weeks every other week. The date is set after spring communion. During the baptism ceremony girls and boys kneel in the center aisle. Girls remove their prayer kapps. As the recipients are baptised in the name of the Father, Son, and the Holy Ghost, a cup holding water is poured upon their heads by the Bishop. The Deacon or Minister assists. A Holy Kiss is given to those baptised by an older woman—no one specific or of any particular importance.

The Holy Kiss in the early Christian church was practiced as a symbolic greeting of a brotherhood of Christians (Referred to in Romans 16:15-16). The purpose in baptism is as a greeting welcoming the new baptised members.

---

[6] Hostetler, John A., *Amish Society*. Baltimore, MD, John Hopkins University Press, 1968. pg 34.

Amish Funerals and Cemeteries

The sound of buggy wheels and horses coming into the farm-yard can mean that a message is being delivered by word of mouth. It is one of the few means of notifying relatives, friends, and neighbors of the death of a loved one. This is another time when families and community come together in faith, giving comfort and support. People begin responding immediately. One or two people are appointed spokesmen for the family and also organize and oversee funeral preparations. Families respond by bringing in food, offering child care and cleaning the home where the funeral is to be held, as well as helping with chores and field work. The funeral lunch is planned and prepared. A downstairs room (usually a bedroom) is cleared of furniture and prepared for the casket and viewing.

Morticians are contacted (usually a phone call is made by an English neighbor). In the meantime, the body of the deceased person is put on a wide board placed between two chairs or on a table. A white cloth is placed over the board with the body laid on top. Morticians come to the home for the deceased. After embalming, morticians bring the body back to the home, where the family bathe, dress and prepare it for viewing. In the meantime the Amish construct an oak two-lidded casket. Also a rough box of pine is made to enclose the casket. There are no vaults. The casket has a raised lid at one end for viewing. The person is dressed as he or she would be for a Sunday Service: white lawn prayer Kapps and white aprons over dark dresses are worn by women; white shirts and dark pants and a vest or jacket are worn by men. Women who attend funerals do not wear aprons.

Wakes are held in which a few people sit up with the body overnight. The family views the body the night before the funeral and are also the last to view after the funeral services. There are no eulogies, praise or flowers, because they believe in simplicity both in life and death. The short sermon and Bible verses speak of the "hope to come" and life after death in God's kingdom and watchfulness (Matt 24:36-44).

The body is conveyed to the Amish cemetery on a wagon with the seat raised to accommodate the casket. It is horse-drawn. Not everyone goes to the cemetery; some remain at the house for the funeral lunch since everyone can't be fed at the same time. The family and others go to the cemetery for short services. There is singing and people respond to words spoken by the Bishop.

Returning to the house after graveside services, the funeral and visiting continue. Later many stay to put the house back in order, folding up church benches and replacing furniture. People continue to be supportive in any way that is needed.

There are two Amish cemeteries serving as burial grounds. The Amish make their own cement markers and engrave the name, date of birth, and date of death. They also mark the years, months, and days the person lived, for example, 56 years, 2 months, 3 days. There are no family plots; the next space is for the next person to die.

Amish cemeteries are on private Amish-owned property; they are small and the stones are close together. The area is fenced off. Mowing is not necessary because there is no lawn. Grass seed is planted to keep weed growth down and to hold the earth, preventing erosion. Weeding and some spraying are done. Deaths, along with births and marriages, are registered at the county courthouse.

After a recent death in the community, I was expressing my sympathy for those family members of the deceased. I was told, "We should feel worse at a birth than at a death." Then I was told, "Think about it for awhile." I can understand the concept. Life in God's kingdom should be preferable to the struggles in life.

In this Amish Community if both parents are taken in death the children are taken care of by the extended family. They would not permit their children to be adopted out into the English world.

In keeping with state laws regarding burial, the Amish do embalm and use a rough box made of pine as an outer burial container to receive the oak casket. (Usually individual English cemeteries have by-laws governing the use of vaults. These rules often require that a vault be used in order to make maintenance of the cemetery easier by preventing the settling of the earth above the burial site. Minnesota state law does not require the use of vaults.)

In this Amish community of Southeastern Minnesota there have been 23 deaths, three of which were accidental, since 1974.

Accidental Deaths

One young man lost his life in a windmill accident. The windmill was being taken down to be repaired. The ground was frozen and spring work had not yet begun. The wheel and axle of the windmill are usually removed to lessen the weight on bringing it down. It was almost to the ground when the men lost control and it dropped to the ground. Most of the men got out of the way as it dropped, but one man hung on too long. It was said by other young men that this man had great strength in his upper body. However, no strength could endure such weight and, as it fell, it threw him into the air like a rag doll. He fell to the frozen earth and was killed instantly. The young widow was left with small children. Family members and church community gave encouragement and support, as is common in this community.

Another accidental death took the lives of two small Amish girls ages three and four. The children were playing with matches in an upstairs bedroom and accidentally set a fire. The girls became frightened and went into a closet. The fire department was called but resuscitation efforts were unsuccessful; the children died of smoke inhalation. They were from a family of eleven. A year later I visited this same home. The father told me "Today is the day we lost our little girls in the fire just a year ago." I realized that for him each individual child could not be replaced or forgotten, no matter how many children there were in the family.

In the fall of the year, when I visited the same family in mid-afternoon, I witnessed the following scene: The children were returning home from school. The young mother said, "Here come my little scholars." It was report card day. She was sitting at the long harvest table, a baby in her arms, on a bench with no back with two or three other preschool children standing around her. We had been visiting in English, but as the children came in she began speaking to them in German, taking time to look at each report card and visiting with each of them. It was as if a curtain had been dropped over me and I was no longer there. Her attention was totally for her children. I sat watching, enjoying this scene.

Soon the children went about doing their chores, as was expected and accepted. The mother and I began visiting in English once again. But her first priority was her children. Her statement "Here come my little scholars", showed a mother's love. This same mother and her older boys took horse and buggy and, for many days in June of the next year, picked strawberries at a berry farm and apple orchard near the neighboring town of Preston to earn extra income. The closeness I sensed from this family, and the way they pulled together, was very apparent to me.

Deaths since 1979: 5 stillborn, 3 pneummonia, 4 cancer, 2 cystic fibrosis, 1 dwarf (under development), 8 stroke or heart disease and 3 accidental.

Amish Social Life

Barnraisings and Quiltings

Barnraisings and quiltings go hand in hand. At every barn-raising there is a quilt to be done. This is provided by one of the women in the community. In good weather the quilting frame is set up in the yard. Many women and girls sit around the frame with their white prayer kapps bent over the frame busily stitching. It is a sight to behold on a hot summer day as the frame of a new barn is being assembled, the women quilting under a shade tree near the house. At one large barnraising there were three quilts in frames — two smaller ones and a large one. About the time of this particular barnraising I had been visiting with an Amish wife, and she told me that there were three barns and a house to go up in that week. (There had been invitations to four frolics.) I asked, "Why so many at this time?" She replied, "Because it's between corn planting and first crop hay." As it turned out they did have a reprieve — in the form of rain. The house and two of the barns were framed up to be worked on as time permitted. The last and largest of these barns was put up and nearly finished in a day. Many Amish from other areas also came to help.

I was told that when a barn has been destroyed by a crisis, fire or storm, it is called a "free-for-all." Neighbors come to help of their own free-will. Food is brought in by many hands. Not everyone who comes to work stays the entire day but will offer their hands until their own chores call them home. They begin at dawn and work until dusk. When there is no crisis and a new barn is being raised for a family, or a son or daughter recently married, it is called an "invited barnraising." The Amish, since moving here in 1974, have raised or put on large additions to at least 35 barns.

There are Amish men in the area who prepare the wood for building. They cut and mark the lumber for barns by drilling holes for homemade wooden pegs and making a mortise in the lumber so it is ready for framing and assembling. No chain saws are used by this Amish group. Gasoline engines are used to power cement mixers. Wood is purchased at local Amish saw mills; however some purchasing is done at lumber yards for tin, hardware, etc.

One hot summer day there was a barnraising near us. It was a large addition to an already-existing barn. The temperature had

81

risen to over 90°F and the humidity was almost equal to the temperature. The barn was in the full sun from sun-up to sun-down. When visiting with some of the men who had been to the barnraising, I said, "It must have been a miserable day working in that heat. As hot and humid as it was, did anyone get sick?" One older Amish man said, "We headed for the shade often." A young Amish man remarked jokingly, "We Amish are much tougher then you Norwegians." (This area of Northern Iowa and Southern Minnesota has many Norwegians.)

An Amish barnraising.

Because this Amish community is small, a barn isn't usually raised in a day. My husband was once invited to a barnraising. He said they were kind enough to help him tear down our old barn and he wanted to reciprocate. Many Amish men came to help and a big job was made small. On the day of the barnraising they began arriving early in the day. The frames were built on the ground and put together with homemade wooden pegs. These frames are raised with manpower, ropes, and pulleys. If it is a large wall, horses, ropes, and pulleys are used. Many men helped lift the frame to a standing position with push-poles. These push-poles are made from the Poplar tree and have a short point on one end. About 30 are used, some short, with the longest being 18 to 20 feet long. Metal sheeting, nails and tin roofing are used to cover the wood frame.

At noon a large meal was served nearby. Everyone sat on benches at long harvest tables. On each plate was a slice of homemade bread. Before the meal they bowed their heads in silent prayer. Then chicken, mashed potatoes, dressing, gravy, vegetables, homemade jams, frosted cakes and pies were served. No one went away hungry! At the end of the meal a bowl of candy bars was passed as a special treat. The meal was served by the women and young girls. When the men had gone back to work, the women cleaned up and then returned to the quilting project which they had started that morning. By the end of the day the quilt was nearly finished as was the barn.

Quilts

Women have a quilt frame set up most of the time, usually near a window where there is good light. One Amish neighbor has quilted more than 200 quilts since coming here from Ohio some 14 or 15 years ago. She sits at her frame quilting many hours a day. This is her way of supporting herself. The quilting frame is rarely without a beautiful colorful quilt. She has also repaired many antique quilts.

Women make the colorful quilts for Englishers. "Their" quilts are of the same colors they are seen wearing: black, dark greens, burgundys, and blues. Cushions for chairs are sometimes quilted of these same dark colors using any of an assortment of patterns.

Quilting Bees are sometimes arranged for families or friends who are experiencing a hardship concerning health or are in a time of crisis. They do not pay into social security or believe in health, fire, or life insurance. These quilts are made and sold (usually to Englishers, stores, tourists or quilt auctions) to help cover medical expenses or other bills. Other members of the community may make other crafts to sell and donate this income also.

Life revolves around the home, so it is understandable how Amish social life shuts out the modern world. Every event that is work-related is called a frolic or bee, which means that it is also a social event. Frolics are events relating to building, for example, a barn frolic; and bees are gatherings of mutual help such as a husking bee, quilting bee, or butchering bee. Visiting and food are a major part of these get-togethers with family and friends.

Birthdays

Birthdays are acknowledged but not necessarily with a gift. Most families celebrate quietly within their own family. However a cake may be made and sometimes there is ice-cream (homemade or from the store). An invitation might come from grandma and grandpa to come for watermelon in the evening for a grand-child's birthday. Adults occasionally plan a visit inviting others for cake for a friend's birthday but this is not a common practice.

Holidays

All church holidays are celebrated but not with the commercial trappings of the outside world. Some of the Christian holidays celebrated are Christmas, Easter, Good Friday, Ascension Day, and Pentecost. Thanksgiving is not a biblical holiday; however some individual families observe it.

A Christmas story: It was December of 1990 and we had had a couple of big snow storms leaving us with ten to twelve inches of snow. That particular day I had decided to take baked goods and candy to my Amish and English friends. The roads were snowpacked and slippery after our wet heavy snow. Trees, bushes and fences as well as telephone wires and poles all held the snow, forming a picture of a winter wonderland. The roads were clear, so with boxes and trays of baked goods in my car I started out. As I drove into one Amish driveway I realized I shouldn't have ventured up this lane. When I reached the yard and went onto the porch of the home, I was greeted warmly and asked into the large kitchen. The smell of the black woodburning stove and the warmth of the room felt good on this blustery day. The straight dark curtains were pulled back and pinned at an angle to let in the daylight. The long harvest table with its white oil-cloth cover stood empty beneath the window, all evidence of the noon meal cleared away.

The Amish father of seven children asked me how I got there. I laughed and replied, "Very carefully." As we visited I noticed, on a homemade stand with casters, that his wife had some jewelry boxes she'd painted black. She had also put a coat of varnish on them. Two shiny black German readers with gold print also lay nearby and those too had been given a coat of varnish. I asked what the jewelry boxes would be used for. (Amish wear no jewelry.) "My girls will use them for sewing boxes and I varnished the boys' German readers to keep them nice." These were to be Christmas gifts. The small gifts they give each other have symbolic meaning in that they are gifts of love.

Christmas is celebrated in the most simple and humble manner, without Christmas trees, wreaths, or any other decoration. I was told that "their" Christmas is celebrated on January 6th which they term the "Real Christmas." It is the twelfth day after "our" Christmas (December 25th). Since the actual date of Jesus's birth is unknown, it was January sixth, Epiphany, that was observed as the feast of Jesus's baptism, with a secondary emphasis on His birth.[7]

Since families are large, getting together can be a problem in preparing room, food and fellowship. Often each separate family will have its own holiday gathering, celebrated with prayer, food, candy, and sometimes gifts. The gifts are simple and practical, and may be either homemade or purchased. Black ice skates were purchased at a secondhand store by one family. Faceless dolls may be given; new homemade clothing, tea sets and dishes are other common gifts for girls. A razor, flashlight, or tools are sometimes given to older boys. Sometimes there may be a larger gift such as a sled to be shared by all the children. One Amish woman gave her sister a colored candy dish full of homemade candy.

The night before Christmas, or early in the morning when the children are still in bed, the parents set the table and place a gift by or on each plate. Sometimes fresh fruit or candy is given. They emphasize that gifts are not always tangible; there are gifts of love just as God gave us His gift of love in the form of His son Jesus. Families get together throughout the Christmas season, which extends from December 25th to January 6th.

---

[7] "Christmas", page 94, vol. 3, *Grolier Universal Encyclopedia*, New York, 1965.

Part III

The Amish and the English

Travel, Communication and Interaction

Amish Leaving and English Joining

Government and State Laws

The Amish and the Local Economy (Tourism and Farming)

Understanding the Amish

Travel, Communication, and Interaction

Traveling by horse and buggy and working fields with draft horses is as natural to the Amish as traveling by automobile is to us. One Amish man even calls his horse an "oatsmobile."

In the Harmony-Canton area we have an Amish shop called Crossroad Buggies where wheelwrights make buggies and sleighs. Most business comes from the Amish community, but Englishers also benefit. The ancient craft of wheelwrights and builders of buggies has been preserved and improved on. Unusual orders come because of tourism; a Florida couple ordered a buggy to be sent by freight to Central America. Another very unusual order came from a prominent government official, the Prime Minister of a small independent country on the Saudi Arabian Peninsula. He was visiting the Mayo Clinic in Rochester and, having time on his hands between appointments, scheduled a tour of the Amish area. He informed the tour guide of his wishes to purchase a buggy as a memento of his visit. Stopping at "Crossroad Buggies," he ordered a buggy stating, "Build it like the one you would build for your Bishop." It was shipped three months later to the capital city of his country.

Crossroad Buggy Shop

Buggy by Buggymaker

The interaction between Amish and English is always present, yet time in many respects stands still for the Amish. Let me explain. They do not have telephones in their homes to interrupt or harass them, or cars to dash about in. However they do live in a modern world so they are confronted constantly with decisions having to do with the necessity and use of telephones and modes of travel that involve bus lines, trains, ambulances, etc. They feel a temporary use of these are not as threatening as conforming to the constant use; therefore they can limit progress and lifestyle.

You may wonder how they get messages and news delivered. They simply rely on the old ways: *The Budget* (a Mennonite-Amish-published weekly paper), word of mouth, letters and notes, and English neighbors. One mother sent a message to me and on the envelope wrote: "School Route." School children are often the messengers who convey notes during the school term. I've received notes and letters signed, ' only me,' 'just me,' and 'your friend.'

Many times Englishers feel overwhelmed by the assistance asked by Amish neighbors, primarily for car transportation. I'm sure this is why the Amish offer money or barter, offering crafts or gifts for services rendered. One Englisher has a van for lease and hires out as their driver for clinic appointments and trips to treatment centers.

One winter the Harmony community came to the aid of an Amish family. Their four-year-old child had been diagnosed with leukemia, needing regular treatments at a hospital in Rochester, about 50 miles away. The parents and child boarded a bus early in the morning, but were not able to get home on the bus until late afternoon. It was a long trip for both parents and child. The Harmony Cancer Support Group became aware of their plight and initiated a helping hand; soon other groups also became involved. Approximately thirty people within our small community were willing to assist, driving, telephoning to meet their needs, and conveying messages to other Amish families.

This line of help runs in both directions. Amish will assist us as well. Englishers have asked those of the Amish community to help with repairing buildings, shingling, tearing down old buildings, assisting with farm work, fencing, etc. Several of our local Amish helped restore the historic Allis Barn near Lanesboro, making it into a resort.

Old Barn Resort - before remodeling.

There are many cases of Amish helping English. For example, in July of 1978 there was a flood in Rochester, MN. Many Amish from this area boarded buses and arrived in Rochester to volunteer their services in cleaning up the destruction and mayhem left in its wake. Another Amish man was a "good samaritan" when he found and got help for an elderly English man who had had an accident on an icy gravel road and overturned his truck in a ditch. The accident was not visible to motorized vehicles going by, but the Amish man passing in his horse and buggy heard the elderly man's cry for help.

Old Barn Resort - after remodeling.

The Amish may travel at a slower pace and have a very different lifestyle but our concerns are alike in wanting to be good neighbors, promoting good relations and having a Christian regard for one another.

Leaving The Amish

When a young adult does decide to "come out," that is, to leave the Amish community, it is difficult for parents and siblings. I feel I must be very careful in speaking of this, as there is already much hurt that is suffered by the family. All they have ever known is a life of self-denial and a life that for generations has been directed towards pleasing God by lifestyle and a Bible-based religion. They feel as badly as we would if we had children who became involved with drugs or alcohol. In fact this statement was made by an Amish person: "You would feel hurt too if your children went a way you didn't approve of." I replied, "You're right, I'm sorry."

Their lives have been family-centered, both in terms of the immediate family as well as in the broader church family. Many people wonder why more young Amish men and women have not left the Amish way. I attribute this to strong family ties. I have asked those who have left why they have chosen to leave. One such person simply told me, "It just wasn't for me."

It is not unusual for Englishers to believe that young Amish boys and girls are naive and innocent about worldly ways. Many who have left this group have remained within close proximity of this community, finding jobs in the small towns nearby. The ways of the world would be quite different in a large city and possibly some sense of security is felt in the rural towns. Since they are used to working, no job is too small or too large. Jobs are found in factories, farms, housekeeping, babysitting, restaurants, hospitals and nursing homes. There is also seasonal work such as picking fruit. One young man works for Dairyland Power Co. as a lineman.

Those who choose to come back into the Amish community are accepted. Those who leave are believed to have fallen from God's favor. In this situation, the Amish practice shunning or *meidung*, which is based on I Cor 5:11: "But rather I wrote to you not to associate with anyone who bears the name of brother if he is guilty of immorality or greed, or is an idolator, reviler, drunkard, or robber—not even to eat with such a one."

The *meidung*, or shunning, is different for those who have been baptised, for they have made a serious commitment to God and the Amish way of life. Baptisms are at age 18 or older. Those who have made this commitment and later leave, therefore, must sit at a separate table. They cannot eat or drink with other baptised adults and are usually seated at a table with the children.

One Amish family member put two tables together, but with a tablecloth over both so it wouldn't be so obvious that the ex-Amish relative was being shunned. Nothing can be taken directly from their hand in food, drink, business, or objects. (Mt 18:16-17 refers to taking witnesses and confrontation, Titus 3:10 refers to warnings, I Cor 5:11 and I Cor 10:21-30 refer to shunning practices).

An ex-Amish who has not been baptised can eat at the same table, but cannot conduct business with an Amish person.

One Amish person told me that, when visiting the home of a relative who is ex-Amish, the Amish person rarely stays over-night. For Amish to stay in an ex-Amish home would be implying approval. It would be preferable to have the ex-Amish relatives visit them in an Amish-related atmosphere.

Some ex-Amish have returned to their previous homes or community for a visit, funeral, or some event and, in order to make their Amish family more comfortable, the ex-Amish relative will dress in Amish-style clothing.

I have never witnessed total shunning, but apparently this varies with each individual family. The rules are very strict; however, forgiveness can be very swift for those who repent. (2 Cor 2:5-11).

After leaving the Amish way, one ex-Amish man bought him-self a bright red sportscar with a sunroof and black leather uphol-stery. It was not too many months later that he was seen at the car wash, washing the motor of a new jeep. I asked him if he had a car and a jeep. He replied, "No, I got rid of that show-off car. This is more practical. I can hunt, fish, and camp out in the jeep." Of course, having been born into an Amish family he was used to a life with people who were practical, hardworking, and very resourceful.

Now he has begun a part-nership with an Englisher couple. They bought a house and remodeled it for a bed and breakfast.

Many Englishers have won-dered why there are not more young people leaving the Amish way. The numbers are extremely small. At the time of this writing (1992) there are 90 families and 339 babies

The old historic Selvig house restored for a Bed & Breakfast by the ex-Amish man and an Englisher.

have been born since the settlement began here in 1974. This is an average of about 5-6 children per family, and only 23 have left.

English Joining The Amish

It is not unusual for young people and adults to write or speak to me about living with an Amish family or to ask about joining the Amish community. They may feel a kinship relating to this lifestyle or romanticize it or feel a religious spirit tugging at their hearts.

I had a conversation with one Amish person who told of an English family who joined their Amish community for approximately 10 years and then left. They decided this life of self-denial and rigid beliefs was not acceptable anymore.

Another time a young English man became acquainted with an Amish man. He eventually went to work with the young Amish man and began dressing and living the Amish lifestyle. The young Englisher's father wanted him to go to trade school so he honored his father's wishes and left his adopted lifestyle. He has now joined a Mennonite group.

I have had people ask, "Aren't they interested in people joining?" No, they are not necessarily interested. They realize that some are curiosity seekers looking for a new experience in life. The Amish also know that good intentions, imagining, and romanticizing (being sentimental and fanciful) and actually living a life of self-denial are different indeed!

Government and State Laws

In the Amish religious community primary allegiance is to God, not to the government. This orientation, therefore, separates the Amish in many ways from the national government and state laws. For instance, the Amish do not participate in government programs such as welfare, social security, or farm programs. In fact, they have a special card exempting them from social security taxes. Even though they do not pay social security taxes, they do pay most other taxes that Englishers do, regardless of the fact that they will not benefit from many of the services provided by these tax dollars. For example, Amish pay a school tax levy even though they do not send their children to public schools. The Amish do not carry insurance. The family and church take care of the needs our insurance policies are meant to cover.

Because of this difference in priorities, the Amish way often collides with English laws. Usually when the Amish beliefs clash with the law it is the Amish who must conform. However, the First Amendment of the Constitution of the United States guarantees that "Congress shall make no law respecting an establishment of religion, or prohibiting the free exercise thereof, or abridging the freedom of speech, or of press; or the right of the people peaceably to assemble, and to petition the government for a redress of grievances."[8]

The Amish want no publicity or arguments with the law; they simply want to live according to their beliefs. It is difficult for us to understand where and why they draw their lines. In explaining to us, they may simply say, "It isn't our way." We may not understand the logic of other religious cultures and why the Amish draw these lines, nor agree with government rulings concerning these religious beliefs but. . . knowing that these same laws protect our own religious beliefs and give us the freedom to be unique individuals in a democratic system should give us great comfort. The Amish Mennonites came to these United States where our laws would protect them because they had been persecuted by the Church of Rome and the Protestant reformers in Europe since the 1500 and 1600s and could find religious freedom here.

One of the more well-publicized conflicts where Amish belief and state law collided is in the court case known as "The Amish

---

[8] U.S. Constitution, 1st Amendment, Bill of Rights.

in Fillmore County vs. The Slow Moving Vehicle Laws of the State of Minnesota." This court case is known in Europe and throughout many of the Amish communities in the United States and Canada. The following explanation is a personal account, pieced together from newpaper articles and from personal conversations.

It is July of 1988, the middle of a three-year drought. In his jail cell the Amish man, jailed for not displaying the slow moving vehicle (SMV) sign on his buggy, can hear the rumble of thunder. He steps up on a ledge and pulls himself up to the small barred window above. He can see the rain coming down, giving the thirsty parched earth much-needed moisture. Even in his strife he can see the blessings being bestowed by a loving Father. The drought has been long.

The jailed man, Gideon Hershberger, is small in stature with a cherub-like face. He has gray, wisplike hair and a long beard. He is a family man with thirteen children. The farm he lives on, approximately 160 acres, supports three families, including those of a farmer, a furniture craftsman and his own, a window maker. He told me about his experiences with jail and the court.

He has been ticketed many times for not displaying the orange SMV sign, paying a few fines but mostly not. The county sheriff's office has given him a final warning: unless he pays his fines he will go to jail this time. In Ohio some 50 years ago it was Gideon Hershberger's father who went to jail because of a school issue. The Amish have objected to displaying the SMV sign, believing it would be putting their faith in objects rather than in God. It is also considered a symbol of the English world. There are at least 14 members of the Old Order Amish in the Harmony community who have been ticketed for not displaying the SMV sign since objection to the usage surfaced in 1985.

After being warned he has another restless night, deciding to go to the County Sheriff's office the next day. When he arrives in Preston, Sheriff Don Gudmundson is not there. Gideon tells me, with a smile, that the deputies told him to go home, "But don't tell anyone we wouldn't keep you. Don will come for you."

Hershberger returns home for another sleepless night. Don Gudmundson arrives the next day to take him into custody. Hershberger asks if he has time to get some clothing, and the sheriff tells him that a pair of coveralls are provided. The overalls are bright orange prison clothes — the same color as the SMV sign. The Amish man states his preference for wearing his own clothing and is allowed to do this. With his black satchel in hand, containing his Bible and clothing, he gets into the patrol car and is taken to Preston.

The time arrives for Gideon to appear before District Judge Margaret Shaw Johnson. He tells it this way: After he sits down "close beside her" (in the witness box), she asks him if he wants to go through with this. She gives him three choices: $150 fine, 30 hours of community work, or 7 days in jail. He says, "I am slow in answering," and finally replies that going to jail is the least he could do for the Amish faith. He tells me, "She, too, was slow in answering." She delivers his seven-day sentence.

Gideon may have become an advocate and hero among the Amish but at what cost?! The Englishers who live nearby, around this Amish-populated area, could not understand flaunting rules of road safety and felt as strongly on the opposing side. They were concerned about both the safety of Amish families and their own because of visibility problems at night and in bad weather, and also because they (the Englishers) are required by law to display the signs and do so.

A long debate was about to begin. The Amish lost their case in the Fillmore County MN District Court in December, 1988. Their attorney appealed, and immediately the Court of Appeals turned the question over to the Minnesota Supreme Court. In August of 1989 the MN Supreme Court ruled that the Amish can, because of religious beliefs, refuse to use the florescent triangular signs and do not have to use an alternative.

The county attorney appealed to the U.S. Supreme Court, which ordered the state court to re-examine its decision in the light of a new ruling (April 1990) which said that states do not have to exempt people from religiously neutral laws when those laws conflict with a religion. The following article, written in November, 1990, for the *Minneapolis Star Tribune* by Bill McAuliffe, a staff writer with an interest in the Amish, sums up the arguments and final MN Supreme Court decision clearly:

"For the second and apparently final time, the Minnesota Supreme Court has decided that the state's Amish residents are exempt from a state law that they say conflicts with their religion.

"In a decision that one justice said is the first clear articulation of the state Constitution's 'liberty of conscience' provision, misdemeanor charges against 14 Amish from Fillmore County will be dropped.

"That brings an apparent end to a controversy that has troubled Fillmore County for much of the past decade and has seen three Amish men jailed, one for nearly a week in 1988. . . .

"The conflict stemmed from the refusal by some members of the Old Order Amish community to use orange slow-moving vehicle warning triangles on their horsedrawn wagons and buggies.

"The agrarian, plain-living Amish have said they interpret the Bible to prohibit the use of bright colors or 'wordly symbols.' But county officials argued that public safety, and Minnesota law, required the use of the signs. Many residents of Fillmore County, including dozens in a tractor demonstration in September, said the black Amish vehicles are difficult to see on county highways, particularly at night.

"In its decision. . . the Supreme Court ruled that the state had failed to prove that red lanterns and an outline of white reflective tape on Amish vehicles are not sufficient for public safety.

"But the court went further to state that where religion and public safety conflict, the state Constitution 'precludes even an infringement on or an interference with religious freedom'.

"'The framers of the state Constitution,' wrote Chief Justice Peter Popovich, 'acknowledged religious liberty as coequal with civil liberty,' and brought to the state more extensive protections of religious practice than those afforded by the U.S. Constitution.

. . .

"'This decision strikes the bell of religious freedom for all citizens,' said St. Paul attorney Phil Villaume, who took the Amish case more than two years ago, free of charge, after reading of the jailing of one Amish man. 'Its impact is far greater than on the Amish. It says it's OK to be different in Minnesota, that people with a different way of life can contribute to our communities.'

"'It also says 'Enough is enough,' that citizens should make every effort to get along,' Villaume added.

"Fillmore County officials said they were frustrated with the decision.

"'I don't think the court considered some of the things we asked them to consider, but there's also a certain amount of relief in saying 'OK, now they've spoken, this is the end', said County Attorney Bob Benson. 'Now we have to try to push something together that all sides can live with.'

"The state Supreme Court decided in favor of the Amish in August 1989, basing that ruling on the U.S. Constitution, and specifically declining to interpret the State Constitution. That decision also allowed Fillmore County to appeal to the U.S. Supreme Court.

"In April the federal court ruled in an Oregon case that some religious practices can be curtailed in the face of a religiously neutral law, and sent the Amish case back to Minnesota for reconsideration.

"Villaume, aided by Hamline University law professors Joe Daly and Howard Vogel, argued that the case could be decided solely within the boundaries of the state Constitution. The state Supreme Court did just that.

. . .

"Attorneys on both sides of the Amish case said they were planning to meet with the Amish to work out some form of reflection for their vehicles that will satisfy both the Amish and their neighbors.

"However, several years ago a special law was passed providing for a black-and-white triangle that the Amish could use. But some Amish continued to resist that. . . ."[9]

Since the court case was decided, the Amish have used neither the bright orange nor the black and white SMV sign. Some have, however, used reflective tape or bars on their buggies, wagons, and other horse-drawn vehicles.

In conclusion, it is appropriate to mention a comment from Doug Meikheim, a professor from the University of St. Thomas, who led an executive seminar group which toured the Amish community in Harmony. He stated that one of the positive views they gained from the visit was that, "Harmony, as a small town,

---

[9] McAuliffe, Bill, "Minnesota Supreme Court reaffirms Amish rights in the SMV traffic case," *Record-News-Republican-Leader*, (reprinted with permission of *Mpls Star Tribune*), Wed, Nov 14, 1990, pg. 1.

has an example to offer the world. Two cultures existing at opposite ends of the poles have learned to exist in a harmonious atmosphere, not without problems, but learning to solve problems within the law and community without wars and in a peaceful manner. Harmony, Minnesota, is unique."[10]

---

[10] Phone interview with Douglas Meikheim, Adjunct professor, University of St. Thomas, St. Paul, MN, April, 1992.

The Amish and the Local Economy

Tourism and Farming

In the early '70s prices were reasonable ($300 to $700) but by the late '70s land prices went soaring to extraordinary amounts of up to $2000 per acre. Interest rates went up from 6% and 8% in 1973 to as high as 21% and 23% in 1981. Speculators also drove farm prices to extremes. Loans were made on these inflated land prices. It became threatening to farmers nationwide when land prices dropped and the land value was no longer there. Farmers were also suffering from low commodity prices and over-production.

Why did land prices drop? It was because of inflation; money was issued beyond what was justified by the country's tangible resources. People thought that times were going to continue to get better and there were predictions of a rosy future with never-ending good times. People bought and borrowed on these inflated prices believing the predictions. Demand for money drove interest rates higher and higher.

By the 1980s many farmers could not keep up with operational costs or the high interest rates, not because they weren't good farmers or were poor managers — it was just bad timing. Farmers by the thousands were forced from their farms by these high costs.

One day I had an interesting conversation with an older man of the Amish community: We were visiting about the crash and depression beginning in 1929 through the 1930s and the "Agricultural Crunch" and depression of the 1980s. He commented that he believed that the farm community as a whole suffered worse during the "Agricultural Crunch" of the 1980s. He explained, "In the 1930s when we sold three fat pigs live weight, we only got $30, but $30 in the 1930s had more worth." Hogs were (and still are) termed "the mortgage lifter." Why? Because the turnover from birth to market is much faster than that of other livestock, (steers for example), therefore bringing in more income at a steadier rate.

In the 1930s nothing brought much on the market. However in the 1930s, both Amish and English farmed with horses at lower operational costs. In contrast, the 1980s farm machinery prices skyrocketed, so the depression and crash of 1929 through the 1930s was supposedly less threatening.

How do the Amish survive and make it on small incomes? Because they are resourceful and have an ingenuity handed down from their forefathers, and also because they haven't been exposed to the million temptations of our "mall society."

Some Amish had financial problems during the 1980s for the same reasons Englishers did but the numbers were less because of lower operation costs. For example: fuel costs are almost non-existent, horse farming cuts operational costs, and very small quantities of commercial fertilizer and chemicals are used. They raise most of their own horses and livestock, their homes are plain*, they raise and process much of their own food (canning fruits, vegetables, and meats; also smoking meat), and they are not slaves to materialism.

The gasoline and diesel engines have modernized the Amish community in a very limited way. The Amish do believe that they may use basic technology in adapting these engines to fit their lifestyle as long as the technology does not dominate their lives. They adapt stationary engines on steel wheels to grind feed, fill silos, thresh and bale hay. Old tractor motors are used as stationary engines and one Amish farmer uses a Chysler truck motor! In this area some of the Amish use a stationary baler (belt and gas driven) in farm yards. The loose hay is brought to the baler.

Amish stacking loose hay on a hay wagon. The hay is cut and left to dry in long rows in the field. When it has dried sufficiently (wet hay stored in a barn can overheat and cause a fire), a hayloader is hooked behind a wagon pulled by a team of horses. As the wagon and loader are driven over the hay rows, hay is conveyed up onto the wagon where workers stack it up high.

Many of these engines are repaired by a 76 year old Amish man. He has a 6th grade education and an affinity for small engines. He is a self-taught man drawing on his experiences of

---

* See chapter in Unit 2 on Homes and Home Furnishings.

the past and present. Many of his buildings are full of what I would term "junk" and parts from old machinery. All or most of it is usable in making repairs.   He stated, "We thought 20 years ago we'd run out of horse drawn machinery, but we kept making and replacing parts from old machinery." When I asked how he kept track of all the "junk" in the many buildings, he smiled and pointed to his head answering , "I have a computer."

Amish repair shop for small engines.

In the 1960s the Amish began using gas engines for pumping and circulating water to insulated cement tanks in which ten gallon cans of milk were cooled. A newer means of cooling milk was developed in Ohio which agrees with their lifestyle but still limits progress. It consists of stainless steel pipes that are attached to a stainless steel lid which fits onto a ten gallon milk can. Circulating water is propelled through these pipes, cooling the milk faster. Insulated cement tanks of circulating water continue the cooling process. Block ice is also used, cut from ponds and stored in ice houses.

Milking is done by hand, and they sell only grade "B" milk. A new outlet for grade "B" milk has been secured through River Valley Cheese Inc. in Lanesboro, Minnesota. This is one of numerous new businesses which have developed in the Bluff Country area in response to the increase in tourism. To show their good faith and to secure a future for generations to come, a few Amish who are financially stable have invested money in this cheese factory, and others have volunteered their hands, remodeling and getting it established. However, this Amish group will not work in the plant. (Some Amish in other colonies do.)

Besides operating at a lower cost, the Amish, when they are young, will do their financing through families within their own community at a lower interest rate or no interest at all. These are unsecured loans. If families within the community can't help these young people, they are put into contact with an Amish individual of another community who can. Christopher Skaalen, President of the Harmony State Bank, stated, "In actuality the Amish community encourages loans outside the community. Usually those taking loans are middle aged people who have acquired enough collateral to secure loans." [11]

With corporate farming becoming more prevalant, Amish are finding it harder to find farms small in acres. Therefore, once they buy a farm it usually remains Amish owned. Approximately 75% of the Amish in this area farm.

Oat bundles in the hay field. The first year a field is planted for alfafa hay, quick-growing oat seed is also planted to protect the slow-growing, tender alfafa plants. Oats are harvested in midsummer when the small alfafa plants are several inches high and can survive on their own. After cutting the oak stalks, bundles are made from the stalks and left in the field a short time to dry.

Our small town, Harmony, like those of other areas which depended on the rural trade, also suffered side effects of the "Agricultural Crunch," which began when prices began to drop in the 1980s. Many farmers went into bankruptcy or had tremendous setbacks. In giving tours and conversing with people from many areas, I have found that the same thing happened every

---

[11] Interview: Christopher J. Skaalen, President, Harmony State Bank, March 27, 1993.

Corn stalks in a corn field. The stalks are bound together in the field. Later they will be brought in from the fields for the animals.

where. Businesses closed their doors, not necessarily because of bankruptcy, but because of the lack of volume of purchases. When the agricultural crisis was at its peak, Harmony had at least five of its businesses "close shop," and by 1986 Harmony's Main Avenue had eight empty store buildings.

In 1988, on top of the other agricultural problems, this area and the surrounding states suffered a drought. Yields were down but prices were up so most farmers in this area survived. Luckily, in our farm area we received rains at the necessary times so, although crops produced fewer bushels per acre, they were sufficient; not a total loss as in some other areas. Farmers hung on and persevered.

After the Amish moved into this area, our school enrollment dropped, and state aid was reduced. However, school population had been dropping before this. Why? Because English farmers began expanding by purchasing more land. Small family farms were becoming less common. It was also because family size tended to be smaller than it was 25 to 50 years ago. (The Amish moving into the area helped to push schools into pairing and sharing and cutbacks sooner.) This added to the economic

107

problems, creating a time bomb waiting to go off in many small communities. Our small town feared for its survival. Then tourism came into our town and surrounding area.

The Amish view tourism as a two-edged knife. One older Amish man, who no longer farms, said, "I made a living without a tourism dollar." They do not like being stared at or letting people into the privacy of their homes. (This also includes people who want to write books or papers on their lifestyle!) I believe they understand the interest but add it up to curiosity. I feel it is much more than that.

Old fashioned General Store in Henrytown that sells Amish crafts.

Strangers and tourists have a tendency for romanticizing, believing that the Amish life may be more acceptable and more like their ancestors' lifestyle, being simpler, slower paced, less pressured. Family life would be stronger with women staying at home, no outside conflicts, more privacy, etc. However, they do not stop to consider the harshness of riding in open buggies in poor weather, the lack of modern conveniences, or the hardships of this life of self-denial.

The Amish know that tourism has also brought about a demand for their crafts. We have many Amish families who are struggling to make a living and crafts have been a means of paying necessary bills or making farm payments. They are careful in the way their crafts are marketed, (unadvertised) and only persons who are interested in purchasing are encouraged to stop. For example, if curiousity seekers who weren't interested in purchasing or placing an order would visit these shops it would be very disruptive to craftsmen. The Amish home is a place of much activity; crops, gardens, and normal chores must be tended to. Tourism can be disruptive and will only be accepted as long as people are respectful of the beliefs and guidelines set by the Amish community. The normal waiting period for a furniture order is about 1 to 1 1/2 years. Our stores (craft shops) have provided a great outlet for Amish crafts. The Amish do not want tourism to become an entrapment. The question is how to do this?

Michel's store where the Amish tours were started and where Amish crafts can be purchased.

The church community would rather not rely on the income of tourism and has struggled to remain separate from the modern world. This is why the church continues to help families with large hospital bills and in times of crisis. However, it is our English people who have contributed to helping the Amish community (in a direct way) through tourism, auctions, etc. For example, many times the Amish church community will make and sell crafts or a quilt to help families with large hospital bills. The primary purchasers are people outside the Amish community.

Wood craft shop. The father makes cabinets and his 16 year old son makes toys. Note the wagon with steel wheels.

Tourism has been a benefit to the Amish community, but it has also benefited English farm families (wives who do crafts and many part-time and full-time jobs for both men and women).

Our town has had a growth of several businesses and we now have a small village within a village called "The Village Green."

The Village Green includes, left to right, The Village Depot, The Village School, and the Sugarplum House.

110

The Lenora United Methodist Church (pioneer church), the oldest church (finished in 1865) in Fillmore County, is included in the Amish tours.

The Harness craftsman's homestead and shop. Note the large pile of slab wood for the woodburning stoves.

Inside the shop of the shoe cobbler and harness craftsman.

Oil drum used for dipping harnesses and bridles into oil at the harness shop.

In a December, 1988, newspaper interview Harmony mayor Marvin Wilt said, "The city (population 1133) has made some real progress economically in recent years. Part of the improvement is due to a rebounding farm economy." He said, "The Amish tours have played a significant role." Wilt said, "However it would be difficult to attach a dollar value to the industry in Harmony."[12]

[12] "Uneasy Neighbors."Minneapolis Star Tribune, December 16, 1988, page 1B.

Understanding the Amish

Many people cannot understand why the Amish choose to live this "backward" life. However the Amish live this way because they are guided by the Bible and it dictates a way of life for them: To live in the world but not be of the world, (paraphrase of I John 2:15-17)[13] To the Amish this simply means a life of self denial and separation eliminating the many lures, temptations, and entrapments of a modern world. Living without electricity and central heating systems, using horses for farming, and a life of sameness and simplicity helps them adhere to a life of faith and trust. I had a conversation while visiting with an Amish friend during our drought in 1988. My friend is quiet, a man of few words. I inquired, "How many bushels of corn per acre did you get this year?" He replied, "We don't measure." He sat quietly neither explaining nor conversing. I questioned again, "Are you saying that as long as you receive crops to fill a need it is not necessary to measure yields?" He answered, "That's right." He was telling me that the pride we take in the yield is not important or desirable. What difference does it make whether a field yields a surplus of bushels per acre as long as crops fulfill their needs? They are interested only in being self sufficient. . . not feeding the world as we are. They do not register cows or livestock. As long as a cow produces milk and fulfills a need, why register it? The temptations of a modern world and our competitive ways are minimized in the way they live.

It is interesting for me to see how hard the Amish work at maintaining a life of simplicity. I witnessed this when they tore down a silo eighty-feet high and twenty feet across. They tore it down block by block from the inside out and had enough block and silo stays to build three smaller 12'x40' silos. These were more feasible without electricity and self-feeders. However, they cannot take down these silos or remove electricity when first purchasing English farms; they will use the modern silos and a submersible water pump temporarily, but never do they use the electricity in the houses. That is disconnected immediately but not removed from the farm until the contract for deed is fulfilled. Not all contracts were written up like this; however, this is one way English farmers can protect themselves should the farm revert to

---

[13] Bible References from *Harper Study Bible*, Revised Standard Version, edited by Harold Lindsell. NY, Harper and Row, 1962.

them. They would not want farms back with electricity and silos removed.

When the contract for deed is fulfilled windmills go up and submersible pumps come out just as modern self-feeding silos come down. The Amish move backward not forward. This is why they draw lines of limitation in a modern world and why a temporary use is practical and not a double standard. It is hard for Englishers to understand such behavior, but the Amish look at it as a temporary necessity, a way of survival.

Is least progressive so bad? I remember a childhood without television and the convenience of running water. Life in a small town (Mallard, IA) was much slower paced than city living and I did not feel deprived. Fifty to sixty years ago, when horse farming was a way of life, people had large families. Large families provided joy and helped lighten the work. Families were also more social; visiting, humor, the art of communication were the entertainment of all people. Love, sharing, caring, support, comfort, and nurturing in large families brought life into full circle. It was a wholesome, country life with families getting together without all the entrapments of worldly things, enjoying the seasons of nature and family life.

Lifestyles may differ, but we are all children under God's direction, living "in Harmony."

Part IV

Stories and Anecdotes

Stories and Anecdotes

"Relative" Experience at Niagara Cave

Niagara Cave, near Harmony, is one of the largest caves in the Midwest. The Amish regularly take visiting relatives on tour of its depths. (Caves and animals in zoos are believed to be natural (God's) creations and therefore are permitted activities.) This cave was discovered in 1924 when three lost pigs were found in a crevice two feet wide.

After taking a cave tour one Amish man related this story: An Amish man's missing dog was heard when its persistent barking came from a sinkhole on his farm.* He tied a rope to his boy and lowered him into the hole to recover the dog. What a scary experience! The rope was secured correctly to the boy, or he might have had the dilemma of recovering both the dog and the boy.

Never Too Old

One of the care centers for the aged in Rochester, MN scheduled a tour to some of our Amish neighbors near Harmony in 1987. One resident of this care center was Reba Kelly, a cigarette-smoking lady of 104. She had in her earlier years (age 99) been nearly arrested after a neighbor reported that she was stealing flowers from an urn at a shopping center. Rochester Police dropped the charges when it became clear she was only taking plants home for the winter to preserve them for spring replanting. Reba's obituary in the Rochester Post Bulletin refers to her notoriety and the fact that she made several appearances on national television because of her concern for these plants.[14]

Joan Michel, office manager at the Michel Amish Tour office, is one person who remembers her, and on that day in September when Reba came on tour Joan describes their meeting:

---

* A sinkhole is a depression which forms in Karst areas. Sinkholes are formed by the removal of earth beneath the surface by underground waterflow. The surface then collapses, forming a hole.

[14] "Rochester's Celebrity, Reba Kelly, dies at 107." *Rochester Post Bulletin*, Rochester, MN, August 20, 1990, Page 2B,

"I remember when she finally got into the store (the nurse had had to usher her back outside to dispose of her cigarette in the gutter) she told me she was glad to finally get to Harmony to see what all the fuss was about with these Amish tours. She told me the story of her sixteenth birthday when she began smoking cigarettes and drinking coffee. 'Been using both ever since,' she said, throwing her arms up in the air to express her delight in both habits. She was a 'ball of fire!!'"[15]

Shoo-fly Pie Disappointment?!

I had given a bus tour and had accompanied the bus to the Old Barn Resort for our noon meal. The tourists had hoped to have Shoo-Fly Pie because we'd just completed an Amish tour. Instead they were served a delicious buttermilk pie. They murmured their disappointment, so I asked how many had eaten Shoo-Fly Pie. None had, but they thought that since the Amish eat and make a lot of Shoo-Fly Pie, they would have liked to try it. The truth is that very few Amish make this pie. They have other favorites like fruit, custard, and cream pies. After eating the buttermilk pie, many wanted the recipe. The recipe was obtained and shared with the group. Later when I told this story to the Amish, they thought it was humorous.

Shoo-Fly Pie
(More like a cake than a pie.)

4# flour or 12 cups	1# lard or 2 cups and salt
2# brown sugar or 4 cups	

Mix like pie crust and store in tight container.

Method for mixing:

2 cups mix	3/4 cups hot water
3/4 cup molasses	1 teasp. soda (scant)

Blend the molasses, hot water, and soda. Add 2 cups of mix. Pour in 9X9 cake pan (or 8" unbaked pie crust.) Sprinkle one cup of the shoo-fly cake mix crumbs on top. Bake at 350° for thirty to forty minutes.

---

[15] Michel, Joan (Letter) 1993.

Buttermilk Pie

(Amish recipe)
(Served to Bus Group)

1/2 cup sugar	1/2 tsp. baking soda
2 tbsp. butter	1 cup buttermilk
1 beaten egg	1/4 tsp. vanilla
1 tbsp. flour	1 pie shell unbaked

1. Cream sugar and butter, add egg.
2. Mix baking soda with flour. Add to creamed mixture.
3. Add buttermilk and vanilla.
4. Pour onto crust and sprinkle with cinnamon.
5. Bake at 350° for thirty-five minutes.

Who's at Fault?

In giving tours of the Amish country the guide rides in the car or van with tourists who wish to learn more about the Amish. On one occasion a tour guide was directed to a couple standing beside a car. They introduced themselves to one another and decided who would drive the car. After the decision was made they drove throughout the countryside stopping at Amish homes to see or purchase crafts, a trip of approximately 30 miles in all.

When they returned to town the couple got out of the car, after thanking their guide, and walked up the street. A state highway patrolman approached the guide, informing him that this car had been reported stolen. What had really taken place was a mistake of ownership: The couple thought the car belonged to the guide while the guide thought the car was theirs. The young woman who actually owned the car had left the keys in the ignition.

No one was charged in this mix-up. The guide certainly learned a lesson and so did the owner of the car, but the couple taking the tour were never any wiser as to what really occurred.

Black Bonnet

One fall I was visiting with Amish friends (two young women) about a robbery that had taken place in Rochester, MN. I told them that a high-speed chase had begun near Preston and continued through Harmony. It was discovered after the pursuit for speeding began that these men were wanted for a robbery in

121

Rochester. One of the offenders had been caught; however the other man ran into a cornfield. Truthfully speaking, I had no idea where the chase had ended or into which area the man (who was black) had fled, but I told the girls that if they saw a black man trying to stop them on the road, just to keep the horses going. One of the girls remarked jokingly, "I'm not worried. I'll just turn my black bonnet around backwards, and he'll think I'm black too!"

Buggy Business

In an Amish buggy shop there was this sign posted and visible to his customers, "I'M NO BATTERY, PLEASE DON'T CHARGE ME," and a sign that said, "IN GOD WE TRUST, ALL OTHERS PAY CASH." There was also another sign that said, "OFFICE HOURS: OPEN MOST DAYS ABOUT 9 OR 10, BUT SOME DAYS AS LATE AS 12 OR 1. WE CLOSE ABOUT 4 OR 5, BUT SOMETIMES AS LATE AS 11 OR 12. SOME DAYS OR AFTERNOONS, WE AREN'T HERE AT ALL, AND LATELY I'VE BEEN HERE JUST ABOUT ALL THE TIME, EXCEPT WHEN I'M SOMEPLACE ELSE, BUT I SHOULD BE HERE THEN, TOO.

Driveway Too Long

One Amish man, speaking about his long farm lane and the difficulty he had in maintaining it, said, "I'd shorten it but then it wouldn't reach the road."

On Common Sense

Another Amish person was speaking of another person's lack of common sense and stated, "You realize that he's also half a brick short?"

A Play On Words

When inquiring as to how many children were in an Amish man's family he replied, five and one-half dozen. (Five and one-half dozen equal eleven.)

Old Time Animal Remedies

I have collected many old-time remedies for animals. Here are a few used by old timers in days gone by and by Amish farmers for horses and calves:

Founder in horses: (an effective treatment) Tie the horse in a cold mud hole or spring, keeping the feet cool. This is an aid used to recover from founder or laminitis. (Founder or laminitis is the inflamation of sensitive laminae in the hoof of a horse.)

Blood letting for founder: This is a very old remedy. A needle is put into the jugular vein of the neck, letting the blood run until it is bright red. It will be dark in color at first. Seal off hole with a pin and hair from the horse's mane.

Colic in horses: (colic is stomach pains) Insert several raw onions into the rectum. The theory here is that the animal will strain and pass the gas and manure which has possibly created the pain.

Relief of calf scours or diarrhea: Use this recipe to make three dough balls: Three tablespoons flour, one tablespoon soda; mix together and add enough water to make a stiff dough. Give one dough ball at each feeding or until relieved.

I would like to thank one of our local veterinarians, Dr. Andrew Overby, for lending an ear to these remedies. He has jokingly said, "I suppose if the animal lives you'll thank the Lord — but if it dies you'll blame the vet."

Home Health Remedies and Stories

I enjoy telling this story because through this experience my book was sparked (or born). It began with my collection of home remedies.

My interest in the use of home remedies grew from a mere sliver I had acquired under my thumb nail. It had embedded itself deeply under the nail, and in my attempts to remove it, it broke off, leaving most of the sliver. A few days later, I was visiting an Amish friend. While there, I told her of the soreness and inability to remove it. She gave me this simple recipe:

Bread and Milk Poultice

Take a crust of bread (the crust because it holds together best), soak it with milk, place over affected area, cover with plastic wrap, and leave overnight. I am not recommending the use of this remedy, but I must tell you if you are left wondering; the sliver did lay in the crust of bread when I removed it the next morning.

Home remedies have been in existence for hundreds of years and are still in use today. In a world of modern medicine and technology, the Amish still use many of these old time remedies. Modern medicine has benefited by research into many of these recipes which use herbs, roots, bark, blossoms, fruits and vegetables. Recent interest in preservation of our rain forests has kept these plants from disappearing.

My intent is to share with you these interesting remedies, hoping you will enjoy the stories and a trip back into the past. I have been collecting remedies and recipes over a period of four years and have enjoyed visiting and sharing material with my Amish friends. It has been surprising to me to see first hand salves using animal fats as a base, cough syrups using chestnut leaves, turpentine and kerosene remedies. I do not claim any value in their usage, but we do believe that God has provided us with a remedy in the nature of his creation for every disease and condition.

A Story of Homemade Salves

When visiting an Amish family in this community I discovered their use of lard or animal fats in making salves. The uses vary from drawing out infections, as a chest smear for colds and lung fevers (pneumonia), to a soothing ointment for irritations and skin softeners.

On entering one home I smelled the strong odor of what resembled tar or burning rubber. I inquired as to what it was and was told of a salve remedy. The ingredients had to be mixed carefully, I was told, because to mix it hot could cause it to explode. It was a remedy passed on from generation to generation. The following are some recipes containing lard. One uses aspirin and vaseline; a comparable concoction to the lard remedies.

Healing Salve

Aspirin crushed and mixed with vaseline used for cuts, bruises, and minor wounds.

Vicks Vapor Rub Substitute

1 oz rosemary oil
1 oz organium oil
1 oz camphor oil
1 oz hemlock oil

Mix with one pint lard. (Keep away from fire!!)

Bittersweet Salve
(poison — for external infections only)

1. Cut Bittersweet root into 2-3 inch lengths
2. Heat in iron skillet with lard over low heat. Stir until it turns orange.
3. Put into jars

A tea can be made of berries. <u>External use only</u> **Poison!!** Soothing for burns, piles, and hemorrhoids.

Story: Acids!

We have an above-the-ground swimming pool in our back-yard made of harvester silo panels, with a vinyl liner. Because of numerous trees and blowing dirt in the air, we empty and clean the pool every spring. Covering the pool is impossible because of high winds. We use a water-diluted muriatic acid solution and a brush for spot-cleaning the liner. My knees were slightly burned one spring, because I got the solution on the fabric of my jeans.

That evening on the way to a supper club in the area, we stopped at an Amish home. We were to pick up and deliver a baby quilt to a niece. While there I complained of my itching, burning knees. I had used a cortaid ointment, thinking it would relieve the symptoms. My Amish friend reached under her cabinet and brought out a bottle of vinegar and told me to splash some on my knees. I did as she suggested. To my surprise, the burning and itching were relieved with only one treatment.

I related this story on tour shortly after this incident. The couple was from Rochester and had scheduled a tour for a visiting relative. As I related this story, referring to home remedies, she (the wife) reached up and touched her husband's shoulder. (He was driving.) She remarked to him "Can you believe this?" She then turned to me saying, "My husband is a dermatologist." I remarked, "She must have been using common sense and experience as her guide." He said, "Yes, however she was using a pH negative and a pH positive." In other words the vinegar neutralized the muriatic acid. Both are acids!

A Surprise Ending
(Foot and Mouth Disease)

The bus on tour was only half full (about 25 people from California). I felt good this day and the interest being shown in the tour was evident in the questions being asked. At several points of the trip I mentioned my writing endeavor, stories, and experiences relating to this very book, stating that I had chosen to self-publish. I had also made remarks pertaining to my struggles as a new writer and responses I had received from publishers. The Director/Chief Curator on this trip (and spokesman for the group) informed me of the group's interest in purchasing my book. I was astonished that they all were interested. My response was, "Don't you think you'd like to see copies before ordering?" (This book was still in the pre-printing stage).

On returning to the starting point of this two-hour tour, I inquired of the Director, in a private conversation, "I hear there is someone on this bus who is a publisher?" He replied, "They are all publishers, editors, and newspaper people." Was I embarrassed!!

Facts About The Amish of Harmony
(S.E. Minnesota area)

1. Amish Mennonite roots date back to the 1500s in Zurich, Switzerland.

2. Menno Simons, a Catholic priest from Holland, joined the ana-baptist movement in 1536. The Amish broke away from their Mennonite roots in 1693. Jacob Amman was their founder and was a Swiss Mennonite bishop.

3. The Amish believe in adult baptism (Anabaptists) and a life of self denial, renouncing the modern world and its temptations and lures.

4. This group in Southeastern Minnesota is known as "Old Order," meaning least progressive. They have no automobiles or tractors, and no electricity. The first Amish settling here were from Wayne County, Ohio. (They have migrated here from Canada, Ohio, New York, Michigan, and Pennsylvania.)

5. There are four church districts, with one bishop and one deacon for each two districts and at least two ministers for each church district.

6. The fifth faction church (about 14 families) is made up of those who chose to use the colored slow-moving vehicle signs (SMV) on their buggies and wagons while the other church districts argued that they were putting their faith in a sign rather than God. The courts ruled that, for religious reasons, Amish do not have to use the SMV signs or any alternative. None of the Amish use the SMV sign now, but many Amish now choose to use reflective bars or tape on their buggies as a safety precaution.

7. Bishops, ministers, and deacons are not ordained nor do they get paid. They believe that they are commissioned by God to serve.

8. Church, baptism, courtship, weddings, births, and funerals take place in the homes.

9. The Amish call all non-Amish "English."

10. Amish homes have beautiful Amish-made furniture.

11. Homes have bare floors and dark curtains of navy blue.

12. Only cold running water is found in Amish homes. It is heated on wood cook stoves for dishwashing, bathing, and washing clothes.

13. Almost all Amish women sew quilted items or make crafts to sell to "English." This helps to supplement the farm income.

14. The first farm was sold to the Amish in December of 1973 and the family moved onto the farm in March of 1974.

15. Some Amish farms are only thirty to forty acres, but plat maps show the average farm size to be about eighty acres. (75% are farmers.)

16. Most Amish families milk cows and sell grade 'B' milk in milk cans. This milk is used for dried milk and cheese.

17. Springs, circulating well water, and block ice (ice houses) are used for refrigeration and cooling milk. Therefore, the Amish smoke and can meats, vegetables, and fruits.

18. Amish stay on standard time.

19. The Amish have wide doors on their barns because horse-drawn manure spreaders can be pulled straight through.

20. Amish help one another thresh grain, fill silos, and raise buildings (which they call frolics: barn frolic or barnraising, shed frolic, house frolic, depending on what building is being built).

21. Grain is cut with a horse-drawn grainbinder and put into shocks. A threshing crew works to bring in the grain and uses a threshing machine which sits in the barn or at the entry to the barn. It is belt-driven by a stationary engine.

22. Silage is cut with a horse-drawn corn binder. Silo filling crews exchange work or the corn is shocked and fed in bundles or shredded.

23. Corn is picked by hand (quite often by family members), then shoveled into corn cribs. Some Amish grind their corn and blow it into small silos with a stationary engine.

24. A corn shredder is used to remove corn from shocks and to shred the fodder and blow it into the barn or into a pile.

25. Husking bees, butchering bees, quilting bees and building frolics are considered social gatherings to accomplish and share work-related jobs.

26. All machinery has steel wheels.

27. There are seven one-room schools where 1st to 8th grade is taught.

28. Teachers are 8th grade-educated.

29. The Amish believe in no graven images and base this belief on the 2nd commandment (Deut 5:8). Therefore there are no faces on dolls, no mirrors in homes (except for a small mirror for shaving), and no cameras or pictures. **They prefer no pictures of any kind.**

30. Some statistics (from 1995) since settling here in 1974:
    103 families;
    480 babies born;
    29 deaths;
    23 new houses have been built;
    40 barns built (including additions to barns):
    31 have left the Amish community.
    8 schools (2 new schools built in 1993)

Amish are located in 22 states and Canada.

Glossary

(Taken from *20 Most Asked Questions about the Amish and Mennonites*, by Merle and Phyllis Good, Lancaster PA, Good Books, 1979, pages 86-89. A very good resource book.)

ALTERNATIVE SERVICE—Various service projects administered by the church that fulfill government draft obligations, yet do not violate church members' peace positions.

AMISH AID SOCIETY—An organization built on the principle of mutual aid. Church members pay annually into a reserve that is then available when disaster strikes a member.

ANABAPTIST—The nickname meaning "rebaptizer," given to the radical group of "Brethren" during the Protestant Reformation who advocated adult baptism. They believed the church should be a group of voluntary adults, baptized upon confession of faith.

AUSBUND—The hymnal used by many Old Order groups, first published in Europe in 1564. It is a collection of lyrics and verses only; tunes are not printed but transmitted orally.

BAN—The practice of excommunication used as a means of keeping the church pure. The ban, based on I Corinthians 5:11, takes many forms, from members being refused communion to having other members not eat with them, visit, or do business with them. One of the issues over which the Amish and Mennonites split in 1693. The practice is designed to bring a member back into fellowship.

BARNRAISING—The practice of rebuilding with volunteer labor a barn that has been destroyed. Amish and Mennonite men gather for a day of work and socializing to build the bulk of the structure.

BISHOP—An ordained overseer of several congregations within a church district. His role is to coordinate leadership and decision making as well as to officiate at communion, weddings and funerals.

BROADFALL TROUSERS—A style of trousers worn by many Old Order Amish men, that instead of a front zipper has a broad flap of cloth that is buttoned shut.

BUDGET (THE)—A weekly paper that carries news of Old Order Amish communities across North America. Through its regular correspondents, it serves as an effective contact among the scattered groups.

BUGGY—The horse-drawn carriage used for transportation by many Old Order Amish and some Old Order Mennonites. Although specific styles vary from community to community, buggies reflect a common commitment to simplicity and suspicion toward technology held by those who use them.

CAPE—An additional piece of material that fits over the waist of a dress. Worn by most Old Orders and many "conservative" women, it is designed for modesty.

DIARY (THE)—The only Old Order Amish magazine published in Lancaster County. A monthly, it records births, deaths, weddings, weather and farm reports for many eastern Amish communities, and usually includes a historical feature.

ECK—The special corner table in the living room where the Old Order Amish bridal party sits to eat following the wedding.

GROSSDADI HOUSE—The extension added to a home when a married child takes over the farm. Parents move into the new smaller section; the young, growing family occupies the large original part.

MARTYRS MIRROR—The large book of stories of Anabaptist martyrs, originally published in 1660. Full of graphic accounts of Christians dying for their faith, a copy is found in most Old Order homes and many modern ones.

MARTYRS SYNOD—The gathering of early Anabaptists (1527) who laid plans for evangelizing Bavaria. Many were killed as they carried out their commissions.

MENNONITE CENTRAL COMMITTEE—The inter-Mennonite relief organization that supplies food, clothing, community development workers, and financial aid overseas and throughout North America.

MENNONITE DISASTER SERVICE—A network of grassroots volunteers—Amish and Mennonite men, women, and youth—across North America who mobilize during national or local disasters to clean up and rebuild.

MODERN—A descriptive term used by the authors to designate those among the Mennonites and Amish who are more influenced in their primary decision making by what the larger society thinks than by what their faith fellowship believes.

NONCONFORMITY—A belief that Christians are different from the world. These groups have given the concept expression in a variety of ways—distinctive dress styles, modes of transportation, wariness toward technology, living peaceably with all, advocating justice and the ethic of love.

NONRESISTANCE—Love in practice; the ideal of returning good for evil, taught by Christ. Its practical expression means refusing to participate in any war, protesting class and racial discrimination, and for some, protesting nuclear danger and world hunger. It is a peaceful approach to life that has also meant, for many, refusing to file law suits, participate in labor unions, or express anger.

OLD ORDER—A descriptive term used by the authors to designate those among the Amish and Mennonites who take their cues for decision making primarily from their faith fellowship (instead of the larger world.)

PATHWAY PUBLISHERS—An Old Order Amish publishing house in Aylmer, Ontario, that publishes three monthly inspirational magazines-Family Life, Young Companion, and Blackboard Bulletin. In addition they publish schoolbooks (for Old Order schools), story books, adult instructional books, cookbooks, and some historical books in German.

PRAYER VEILING—The head covering worn by women when "praying or prophesying;" an interpretation of I Corinthians 11.

PRIESTHOOD OF ALL BELIEVERS—The Biblical concept that within the church each member is responsible to counsel, discipline and support all other members. Although leaders are believed to be ordained of God, they are selected from the laity and act as servants of the church.

"PUBLISHED"—The announcing of an Amish couple's plans to marry. The announcement is made by a bishop during a Sunday morning service.

"THE QUIET IN THE LAND"—Name given to Anabaptist groups as the movement settled down and many members fled to rural areas.

SCHLEITHEIM CONFESSION OF FAITH—The brotherly agreement arrived at by divergent Anabaptist groups, scattered across Europe, in 1527. It is often credited with unifying the brotherhood sufficiently to save the movement.

SHUNNING—An expression of the ban in which members do not keep company with an offending member who has fallen out of fellowship.

STEEL-WHEELED TRACTORS—Used by some Old Order farmers for field work. The steel wheels remove the temptation to use the tractor for transportation on the road.

VOLUNTARY SERVICE—Church administered projects that allow members to offer from three months to two years of their time for service overseas or at home, without pay.

Bibliography

Periodicals and Newspapers

The Budget, a weekly paper serving the Amish and Mennonite communities throughout the Americas, published in Sugar Creek, Ohio, Sugar Creek Budget Publishers Inc.

Clark's Natural Herbs, PO Box 12, Chaffee, NY 14030. Letter of advertisement, 1990-1991, and catalog of botanicals.

Family Life, Young Companion, Blackboard Bulletin, Amish Periodicals published monthly by Pathway Publishing House, Aylmer, Ontario.

Memories of Early Years of Harmony by Anna Aaberg Jacobson, 1956.

Mennonite Church History Chart, 1890-1960, compiled by Elmer G. Swartzendruber, edited by Lonnie Yoder. Kalona, IA, Erickson and Erickson, 1984. Available from Mennonite Historical Society, Kalona.

McAuliffe, Bill, "Minnesota Supreme Court reaffirms Amish rights in the SMV traffic case." *Record-News-Republican-Leader,* (reprinted with permission of *Mpls Star Tribune*), Wed, Nov 14, 1990, pg. 1.

"Rochester's Celebrity, Reba Kelly, dies at 107." *Post Bulletin,* Rochester, MN, August 20, 1990, pg 2B.

"Uneasy Neighbors." *Minneapolis Star Tribune,* December 16, 1988, page 1B.

Buck, Roy C., "Boundary Maintenance Revisited: Tourist Experience in an Old Order Amish Community." *Rural Sociology,* Vol. 43, No. 2, Summer 1978, pages 221-234.

Books read and/or used as Resource Material

Farm and Home Plat and Directory, Fillmore County, MN. Belmond, IA, Farm and Home Publishers, 1991.

Fisher, Sara E. and Rachel K. Stahl, *The Amish School.* Lancaster, PA, Good Books, 1986.

Good, Merle and Phyllis, *20 Most Asked Questions about the Amish and Mennonites.* Lancaster, PA, Good Books, 1979.

Good, Merle, *Who Are The Amish?* Lancaster, PA, Good Books, 1985.

Grolier Universal Encyclopedia. NY, Grolier Incorporated, 1965. Vol 3.

Harper Study Bible, Revised Standard Version, Edited by Harold Lindsell. NY, Harper and Row, 1962.

Hostetler, John A., *Amish Society.* Baltimore, MD, Johns Hopkins University Press, 1968.

Hostetler, John A., *Amish Life.* Scottdale, PA, Herald Press, 1959.

Kaiser, Grace H., *Dr. Frau.* Lancaster, PA, Good Books, 1986.

Kloss, Jethro, *Back to Eden* (A Herbal Book). Loma Linda, CA, Back to Eden Books, 1946.

Kraybill, Donald B., *The Riddle of Amish Culture.* Baltimore, MD, Johns Hopkins University Press, 1989.

Meyer, Joseph E., *The Herbalist.* Hammond, Indiana, Hammond Book Co., 1934.

Miller, Levi, *Ben's Wayne.* Lancaster, PA, Good Books, 1989.

The One Volume Bible Commentary, edited by Rev. R. Dummelow. New York, MacMillan, 1936.

Pellman, Rachel and Kenneth, *Amish Doll Quilts, Dolls and Other Playthings.* Lancaster, PA, Good Books, 1986.

Pellman, Rachel T. and Joanne Ranck, *Quilts Among The Plain People.* Lancaster, PA, Good Books, 1981.

Ruth, John L., *A Quiet and Peaceable Life*. Lancaster PA, Good Books, 1979.

Scott, Stephen, *The Amish Wedding*. Lancaster PA, Good Books, 1988.

Scott Stephen, *Why Do They Dress That Way?* Lancaster, PA, Good Books, 1986.

Stroll, Joseph, David Luthy, and Elmo Stoll, editors, *Our Heritage* (8th grade reader). Aylmer, Ontario, Pathway Publishing Corp., 1980 (c 1968).

Van Braght, Thieleman J., *Martyr's Mirror*. Elkhart, Indiana, Mennonite Publishing Co., 1886.

Webster's Encyclopedia of Dictionaries, New American Edition, Compiled by John Gage Allee. Ottenheimer Publishers, 1981.

Zielinski, John M., *Amish Horse Farming Across America*. Iowa Heritage Publications, 1988.

Government Documents

Minimum Standards For The Amish Parochial or Private Elementary Schools of the State of Ohio as a form of Regulations. Compiled and approved by Bishops, Committeemen and others in conference, 1992.

Minnesota Dept. of Education, *1991 Education Laws*. Volume I, Chapters 117-125. Extract from 1991 MN Statutes, printed January 1992.

Minnesota Dept of Health, "The Law, Rule and Other Related Materials Pertaining to Health, Morticians, Funeral Directors, Fees and Licensing" (pamphlet). May, 1992.

Minnesota Statutes Annotated. Chapter 301, Private Cemeteries, pages 796-797.

State of MN in Supreme Court, Decision C9-88-2623, November 13, 1990.

U.S. Constitution, 1st Amendment, Bill of Rights.

Interviews and Personal Letters

Abraham, Kenneth (Funeral Director). Telephone and personal interviews, 1991-1992.

Amdahl, Orval, (Fillmore County Recorder). Personal and telephone interviews, 1991-1992.

The Amish of the Harmony Community. Shared writing and personal contact, 1988-1993.

Casterton, Jim (Superintendent of Harmony and Mabel-Canton Schools). Personal interviews, 1991-1992.

Connolly, Jim (Fillmore County Sheriff). Personal interview, 1992.

Craig, Norman (Fillmore County Zoning Administrator). Personal interview, 1992.

Druckenbrod, Pastor Richard (Director, PA German Society). Letters, August, 1992.

Luthy, David (Librarian, Amish Historical Library, Ayler, Ontario, Canada). Letter, August, 1992.

Menikheim, Douglas K. (Adjunct Professor, St. Thomas University). Letter and telephone interview, 1992.

Michel, Joan (Office Manager at Michel Farm Vacations and Amish Tours). Personal interview and letter, 1993.

Ohio Board of Nursing. Letter, May 3, 1992, Photocopy of Ohio Statutes Section 4723.41 to section 4723-45.

Overby, Andrew (Veterinarian, Harmony Veterinary Clinic PA). Personal and telephone interviews, 1992-1993.

Skaalen, Christopher (President, Harmony State Bank). Personal interview, 1993.

Schowalter, Joyce M. (Executive Director, Minnesota Board of Nursing). Letter and Photocopy of Minnesota Statutes 148.30-148.32, 1992.